75-7

The
Least
You
Should
Know
about
English
Writing
Skills

FORM A
Sixth Edition

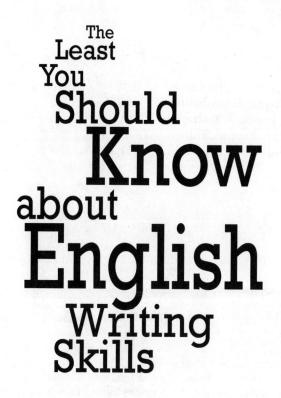

The
Least
You
Should
Know
about
English
Writing
Skills

TERESA FERSTER GLAZIER

Harcourt Brace College Publishers

Fort Worth Philadelphia San Diego New York Orlando Austin San Antonio
Toronto Montreal London Sydney Tokyo

This text is available in Form A, Form B, and Form C so that a different form may be used in various semesters. The three forms are essentially the same except that they have different exercises, writing assignments, and essays.

Publisher	Christopher P. Klein
Senior Acquisitions Editor	Carol Wada
Product Manager	Ilse Wolfe West
Project Editor	Denise Netardus
Production Manager	Serena B. Manning
Art Director	Garry Harman

Harcourt Brace may provide complimentary instructional aids and supplements or supplement packages to those adopters qualified under our adoption policy. Please contact your sales representative for more information. If as an adopter or potential user you receive supplements you do not need, please return them to your sales representative or send them to: Attn: Returns Department, Troy Warehouse, 465 South Lincoln Drive, Troy, MO 63379.

Requests for permission to make copies of any part of the work should be mailed to: Permissions Department, Harcourt Brace & Company, 6277 Sea Harbor Drive, Orlando, FL 32887-6777.

Address for Editorial Correspondence: Harcourt Brace College Publishers, 301 Commerce Street, Suite 3700, Fort Worth, TX 76102.

Address for Orders: Harcourt Brace & Company, 6277 Sea Harbor Drive, Orlando, FL 32887-6777. 1-800-782-4479, or 1-800-433-0001 (in Florida).

ISBN: 0-03-017497-X

Library of Congress Catalog Card Number: 97-70645

Printed in the United States of America

7 8 9 0 1 2 3 4 5 6   016   9 8 7 6 5 4 3 2 1

To the Instructor

This book is for students who need to review the rules of English composition and who may profit from a simplified approach. The main features of the book are these:

1. It is truly basic. Only the indisputable essentials of spelling, grammar, sentence structure, and punctuation are included because research has shown that putting too much emphasis on mechanics is not the way to help students learn to write.
2. It stresses writing. A writing section, EIGHT STEPS TO BETTER WRITING (pp. 188–206), provides writing assignments to be used along with the exercises. The section has been kept brief because **students learn to write by *writing* rather than by reading pages and pages *about* writing.** Even though the section is only 29 pages (compared to 187 for the first part of the text), students will no doubt spend more time on it than on all the rest of the book.
3. It stresses thinking. As students write logically organized papers, they learn that *writing* problems are really *thinking* problems.
4. It uses little linguistic terminology. A conjunction is a connecting word; gerunds and present participles are *ing* words; a parenthetical constituent is an interrupter. Students work with words they know instead of learning a vocabulary they'll never use again.
5. It has abundant practice sentences and paragraphs—enough so that students learn to use the rules automatically and thus *carry their new skills over into their writing*.
6. It includes groups of thematically related, informative sentences on such subjects as a field of diamonds in the United States, pigeon racing, famous people who didn't do well in school, the most popular state birds, two world records set on Mount Everest, the art of juggling, a car that runs on a tankful of sunshine, a walk to the Pole, Henry Ford's first car, the history of pencils, . . . thus making the task of doing the exercises interesting.
7. It provides answers at the back of the book so that students can correct their own work, thus teaching themselves as they go.
8. It includes at the end of the Writing Section five essays to read and summarize. Students improve their reading by learning to spot main ideas and their writing by learning to write concise summaries.

9. It can be used as a self-tutoring text. The simple explanations, abundant exercises, and answers at the back of the book provide students with a writing lab in their own rooms.

Students who have previously been overwhelmed by the complexities of English should, through mastering simple rules and through writing and rewriting simple papers, gain enough competence to succeed in further composition courses.

TFG

A packet of ready-to-photocopy tests covering all parts of the text (four for each section) is available to instructors. Also available is Grammar Tools software that will allow the instructor to send a class to a computer lab for additional practice or for testing. These aids are free upon adoption of the text and may be obtained from the local Harcourt Brace representative or from the Developmental English Editor, Harcourt Brace, 301 Commerce Street, Suite 3700, Fort Worth, TX 76102.

Contents

What Is the Least
You Should
Know?

What <u>Is</u> the Least You Should Know?

Most English textbooks try to teach you as much as they can. This one will teach you the least it can—and still help you learn to write acceptably. You won't have to bother with predicate nouns and subordinating conjunctions and participial phrases and demonstrative pronouns and all those terms you've been hearing about for years. You can get along without them if you'll learn thoroughly a few basic rules. You *do* have to know how to spell common words; you *do* have to recognize subjects and verbs to avoid writing fragments and run-together sentences; you *do* have to know a few rules of punctuation—but rules will be kept to a minimum.

Unless you know these few rules, you'll have difficulty communicating in writing. Take this sentence for example:

Let's eat dad before we start our trip.

We assume the writer isn't a cannibal but merely failed to capitalize and put commas around the name of a person spoken to. If the sentence had read:

Let's eat, Dad, before we start our trip.

then no one would misunderstand. Or take this sentence:

Max said the police officer was driving without a license.

Do police officers usually drive without a license? Perhaps the writer meant:

"Max," said the police officer, "was driving without a license."

Punctuation makes all the difference. What you'll learn from this text is simply to make your writing so clear that no one will misunderstand it.

The English you'll learn to write is called standard English, and it may differ slightly from the English spoken in your community. All over the country, various dialects of English are spoken. In northern New England, for example, people leave the r off certain words and put an r on others. President Kennedy said *dollah* for *dollar, idear* for *idea,* and *Cubar* for *Cuba.* In some communities many people leave the s off some verbs and put an s on others, saying *he walk* and *they walks* instead of *he walks* and *they walk.*

But no matter what English dialect people *speak,* communication is made easier when everyone *writes* the same dialect—standard English. You can say, "Whacha doin? Cmon," and everybody will understand, but you can't *write* that way. If you want your readers to understand what you write, you'll have to write the way English-speaking people all over the world write—in standard English. Being able to write standard English is essential in college, and it undoubtedly will be an asset in your career.

It's important to master every rule as you come to it because many rules depend on previous ones. For example, unless you learn to pick out subjects and verbs, you'll have trouble with run-together sentences, with fragments, with subject-verb agreement, and with punctuation. The rules are brief and clear, and it won't be difficult to master all of them . . . *if you want to.* But you do have to want to!

Here's the way to master the least you should know:

1. Study the explanation of each rule carefully.
2. Do the first exercise (ten sentences). Correct your answers using the answer section at the back of the book. If you miss even one answer, study the explanation again to find out why.
3. Do the second exercise and correct it. If you miss a single answer, go back once more and study the explanation. You must have missed something. Be tough on yourself. Don't just think, "Maybe I'll hit it right next time." Go back and master the rules, and *then* try the next exercise. It's important to correct each group of ten sentences before going on so that you'll discover your mistakes while you still have sentences to practice on.
4. You may be tempted to quit when you do several exercises perfectly. Don't! Make yourself finish every exercise. It's not enough to *understand* a rule. You have to *practice* it. Just as understanding the strokes in swimming won't help unless you actually get into the pool and swim, so understanding a rule about writing isn't going to help unless you practice using it.

   If you're positive, however, after doing five exercises, that you've mastered the rules, take Exercise 6 as a test. If you miss even one answer, you must do all the rest of the exercises. But if you get Exercise 6 perfect, then spend your time helping one of your friends. Teaching is one of the best ways of learning.

5. But rules and exercises are not the most important part of this book. **The most important part begins on page 188—when you begin to write.** The Writing Assignments, grouped together in the back of the book for convenience, are to be used along with the exercises. At the end of most chapters in the front part of the book, you'll be referred to the Writing Assignments in the back. Also you'll sometimes be asked to do another kind of writing—Journal Writing, which calls for just a few sentences in your daily journal using the rules you've learned that day.

Mastering these essentials will take time. Generally, college students are expected to spend two hours outside of class for each hour in class. You may need more. Undoubtedly, the more time you spend, the more your writing will improve.

Spelling

1

1 Spelling

Anyone can learn to spell. You can get rid of most of your spelling errors by the time you finish this book if you want to. It's just a matter of deciding you're going to do it. If you really intend to learn to spell, master the first seven parts of this section. They are

YOUR OWN LIST OF MISSPELLED WORDS
WORDS OFTEN CONFUSED
USE OF APOSTROPHE: CONTRACTIONS
USE OF APOSTROPHE: POSSESSIVES
WORDS THAT CAN BE BROKEN INTO PARTS
RULE FOR DOUBLING A FINAL CONSONANT
USING YOUR DICTIONARY

Master these seven parts, and you'll be a good speller.

YOUR OWN LIST OF MISSPELLED WORDS

On the inside back cover of this book, write correctly all the misspelled words in the papers handed back to you. Review them until you're sure of them. That will take care of most of your errors.

WORDS OFTEN CONFUSED

By mastering the spelling of these often-confused words, you'll take care of many of your spelling problems. Study the words carefully, with their examples, before trying the exercises.

a, an

Use *an* before a word that begins with a vowel *sound* (*a, e, i,* and *o,* plus *u* when it sounds like *uh*) or silent *h*. Note that it's not the letter but the *sound* of the letter that matters.

an apple, an essay, an icicle, an onion
an uproar, an umpire (the *u*'s sound like *uh*)
an hour, an honest man (silent *h*)

Use *a* before a word that begins with a consonant sound (all the sounds except the vowels, plus *u* or *eu* when they sound like *you*).

a pencil, a hotel, a history book
a union, a uniform, a unit (the *u*'s sound like *you*)
a European trip, a eulogy (*eu* sounds like *you*)

accept, except

Accept is a verb and means "to receive willingly."
(See p. 55 for an explanation of verbs.)
I *accept* your invitation. (receive it willingly)
Except means "excluding" or "but."
Everyone came *except* him. (but him)

advise, advice

Advise is a verb (pronounce the *s* like *z*).
I *advise* you to try again.
Use *advice* when it's not a verb.
That's good *advice.*

affect, effect

Affect is a verb and means "to influence."
Her advice may *affect* his decision.
Effect means "result." If *a, an,* or *the* is in front of the word, then you'll know it isn't a verb and will use *effect.*
His words has a great *effect* on the crowd.
The rain had no *effect* on the attendance.

all ready, already

If you can leave out the *all* and the sentence still makes sense, then *all ready* is the form to use. (In that form, *all* is a separate word and could be left out.)

I'm *all ready* to go. (*I'm ready to go* makes sense.)
Lunch is *all ready*. (*Lunch is ready* makes sense.)

But if you can't leave out the *all* and still have the sentence make sense, then use *already* (the form in which the *al* has to stay in the word).

I'm *already* late. (*I'm ready late* doesn't make sense.)

are, or, our

Are is a verb.
We *are* going to win.
Or is used between two possibilities.
You may go now *or* later.
You may have tea *or* coffee.
Our shows we possess something.
Our car needs a tune-up.

brake, break

Brake used as a verb means "to slow or stop motion." It's also the name of the device that slows or stops motion.
You *brake* to avoid an accident.
You slam on your *brakes*.
Break used as a verb means "to shatter" or "to split." It's also the name of an interruption, as "a coffee break."
You *break* a dish or an engagement or a record.
You enjoy your Christmas *break*.

choose, chose

I will *choose* a partner right now.
I *chose* a partner yesterday.

clothes, cloths

Her *clothes* were attractive.
We used soft *cloths* to polish the furniture.

coarse, course

Coarse describes texture, as *coarse* cloth or *coarse* hair.
The material in his suit was *coarse*.
Course is used for all other meanings.
Of *course* I enjoyed the geology *course*.

complement,
compliment

The one spelled with an *e* comple_t_es something or brings it to perfection.

A 30° angle is the *complement* of a 60° angle.
Her blue scarf *complements* her gray suit.

The one spelled with an *i* has to do with praise. Remember "*I* like compliments," and you'll remember to use the *i* spelling when you mean praise.

I appreciated the *compliment.*
She *complimented* him on his new job.

conscious,
conscience

Conscious means "aware."

I wasn't *conscious* that he had left.

The extra *n* in *conscience* should remind you of NO, which is what your conscience often says to you.

My *conscience* told me not to cut class.

dessert, desert

Dessert is the sweet one, the one you like two helpings of. So give it two helpings of *s.*

We had apple pie for *dessert.*

The other one, *desert,* is used for all other meanings and has two pronunciations.

He'll never *desert* her.
The camel moved slowly across the *desert.*

do, due

You *do* something.

I always *do* the best I can.

But a payment or an assignment is *due;* it is scheduled for a certain time.

My term paper is *due* tomorrow.

does, dose

Does is a verb.

He *does* his job well. He *doesn't* take time off.

A *dose* is an amount of medicine.

That was a bitter *dose* of medicine.

feel, fill

Feel describes your feelings.

I *feel* sleepy.

Fill is what you do to a cup.

Will you *fill* my cup again?

fourth, forth

The word *fourth* has *four* in it. (But note that *forty* does not. Remember the word *forty-fourth.*)

This is our *fourth* game.

That was our *forty-fourth* point.

If you don't mean a number, use *forth.*

She walked back and *forth.*

have, of

Have is a verb. When you say *could have*, the *have* may sound like *of*, but it is not written that way. Always write *could have, would have, should have, might have.*

I should *have* finished my work sooner.
Then I could *have* gone home.

Use *of* only in a prepositional phrase (see p. 61).

I often think *of* him.

hear, here

The last three letters of *hear* spell "ear." You *hear* with your ear.

I can't *hear* you.

The other spelling *here* tells "where." Note that the three words indicating a place or pointing out something all have *here* in them: *here, there, where.*

Where are you? I'm right *here.*

it's, its

It's is a contraction and means "it is" or "it has."

It's cold. (It is cold.)
It's been cold all week. (It has been cold . . .)

Its is a possessive. (Possessives such as *its, yours, hers, ours, theirs, whose* are already possessive and never need an apostrophe. See p. 33.)

The committee gave *its* report.
The cat licked *its* paws.

knew, new

Knew has to do with knowledge (both start with *k*).
New means "not old."

He *knew* he wanted a *new* job.

know, no

Know has to do with knowledge (both start with *k*).

I *know* what I want.

No means "not any" or the opposite of "yes."

I have *no* time. *No,* I can't go.

EXERCISES

Underline the correct word. Don't guess! If you aren't sure, turn back to the explanatory pages. When you've finished ten sentences, compare your answers with those at the back of the book. Correct each group of ten sentences before continuing so you'll catch your mistakes while you still have sentences to practice on.

□EXERCISE 1

1. This fall we've been decorating the (knew new) house we just bought, and we like the (affect effect) we're getting.
2. (It's Its) more fun to decorate on your own than to (accept except) the (advice advise) of (a an) interior decorator.
3. First, of (coarse course), we painted all the walls a light beige.
4. Then we were (conscience conscious) that we needed some (knew new) furniture.
5. We bought some chairs to (complement compliment) the sofa we (all ready already) had.
6. Then we (choose chose) some (knew new) drapes for the living room.
7. Finally we hung our pictures, but we had so many that it was difficult to (choose chose) among them.
8. Then we turned (are our) attention to the outdoors.
9. We decided to plant some colorful shrubs around the house to (brake break) the monotony of the all-green lawn.
10. Now we (feel fill) completely satisfied, and I (do due) think (it's its) the best property we could ever (have of) found.

□EXERCISE 2

1. I never (knew new) before that salt played (a an) important part in the history of the earth.
2. Animals wore paths to salt licks, and of (coarse course) people followed, making trails and then roads.
3. When people began to eat grains, they needed more salt, and salt became (a an) essential item of trade.
4. In the sixth century, merchants in the Sahara (desert dessert) traded salt ounce for ounce for gold.
5. I never (knew new) that cakes of salt were at one time used as money in central Africa.
6. As part of their pay, Roman soldiers were given a salarium (money to buy salt), and from that word we get (are our) word *salary*.
7. In New Testament times, (know no) greater (complement compliment) could be given to anyone than to say, "Ye are the salt of the earth."
8. In eighteenth-century England, a silver salt container was placed in the middle of a long dining table, and the host (choose chose) his most important guests to sit with him "above the salt." Less important people sat "below the salt."
9. Over three pages of the *Oxford English Dictionary* (are our) devoted to salt—more pages than for any other food.
10. For centuries even a grain of salt was valuable, but of course (it's its) worthless now.

□EXERCISE 3

1. Last summer I (choose chose) to spend all (accept except) a few days of my vacation in Toronto.
2. It was a (knew new) experience, and I (all ready already) want to go back.
3. It was (a an) excellent (brake break) from my life (hear here).
4. (It's Its) a great city and well worth visiting.
5. It (doesn't dosen't) have slum areas, and it has interesting places to visit.
6. On the (advice advise) of a friend, I went first to the CN Tower.
7. (It's Its) one of the tallest freestanding structures ever built.
8. I rode in a glass-faced elevator to the world's highest observation deck, where I walked back and (forth fourth). The views (are our) breathtaking.
9. Of (coarse course) I had lunch in the revolving restaurant and could look out through the glass walls for a hundred kilometers as I ate my (desert dessert).
10. Then I had (a an) equally interesting experience in the afternoon.

□EXERCISE 4

1. I (choose chose) to visit "Honest Ed's World Famous Bargain House."
2. Ed Mirvish started his store in 1948 with (a an) ad that said, "Our building is a dump! Our service is rotten! Our fixtures are orange crates! But!!! Our prices are the lowest in town!"
3. The (affect effect) of the ad was that the crowds rushed in, and of (coarse course) the enterprise grew.
4. It now includes a block-long group of restaurants that can serve more than 2,500 customers at a single sitting.
5. The Bargain House opens at 11, and I (hear here) that on cold mornings Mirvish sends coffee out to those waiting in line.
6. Slogans (are our) everywhere in flashing lights: "Honest Ed is for the birds. His prices are cheap, cheap, cheap!"
7. Mirvish doesn't (do due) any planning ahead. He says, "I just get up in the morning and let the day unravel around me."
8. I (hear here) that the mayor of Toronto called Honest Ed's a "key part of life in Toronto."
9. After finding a couple of bargains on (cloths clothes) I needed for school, I (knew new) I had (know no) more time to spend.
10. My Toronto visit was one of my best vacations, but I (do due) wish I could (have of) been there when the Toronto Maple Leafs were playing.

☐EXERCISE 5

1. I've been reading (a an) excellent chapter in my astronomy text about the size of (are our) universe.
2. Of (coarse course) I (all ready already) (knew new) that (it's its) immense.
3. I wasn't (conscience conscious) though of (it's its) real size.
4. I should (have of) learned all this earlier because (it's its) (a an) important part of one's education.
5. I (knew new) that we live in the Milky Way galaxy.
6. But I didn't (know no) that (it's its) 100,000 light-years in diameter.
7. A light-year is six trillion (6,000,000,000,000) miles—(a an) unimaginable number.
8. And the Milky Way is by (know no) means the largest galaxy.
9. I now (know no) the names of some constellations, and it (does dose) make looking at the night sky more interesting.
10. I'm glad I (choose chose) this astronomy (coarse course), and I'm (all ready already) planning to take another.

☐EXERCISE 6

1. Last summer at the Museum of Science and Industry in Chicago I saw (a an) unusual movie about beavers.
2. It was in the Omnimax Theater. (It's Its) a "surround" theater in which the audience seems to be right in the center of the action.
3. The (affect effect) is amazing.
4. Until I saw that movie, I never (knew new) much about beavers (accept except) that they (are our) the largest North American rodents and that they build dams across streams.
5. The narrator began by saying, "This is the biggest dam movie you (are our) ever going to see."
6. The movie then showed two beavers cutting down trees to make logs to (brake break) the flow of a little stream.
7. One beaver gnawed through (a an) acacia tree.
8. As the tree came crashing down, it seemed as if it was going to land right in (are our) laps.
9. A beaver's four prominent front teeth (are or) constantly growing because they (are our) continually being worn down by gnawing on the tree trunks.
10. In the (coarse course) of one season two beavers can cut down over one hundred trees.

☐EXERCISE 7

1. After the beavers had enough logs to stop the flow of the stream, they of (coarse course) cut more logs to make their dam.
2. Then through the dam they dug a (knew new) tunnel that led to their warm, dry chamber above the water level.
3. This dry chamber was a dome-shaped lodge of sticks plastered with mud with one (are or) more entrances below the water level.
4. In this dry chamber above the dam little beavers (are our) raised on a bedding of grass and leaves.
5. For a while they ride on their parents' backs, but finally after two (are or) three years they of (coarse course) begin to learn their parents' skills.
6. The beavers alter the surface of the earth more than any other creatures (accept except) humans.
7. What the beavers (do due) is beneficial to the environment.
8. The large pond above the dam becomes home to many (knew new) plants and animals, and the small pond below is also home to different plants and animals.
9. The beaver dam may stand for one hundred years.
10. And the land above and below it will be fertile because of (it's its) transformation by the beavers.

☐EXERCISE 8

1. I (hear here) that a citizens' conservation group—the American Forestry Association—has launched a (knew new) project called Global Releaf.
2. Global Releaf has undertaken a campaign to plant 100 million (knew new) trees in American cities and towns, and a number of states have (all ready already) agreed to participate.
3. California has pledged to plant twenty million trees by the year 2000, and I (know no) that the mayor of Los Angeles has pledged to plant five million in the Los Angeles area alone.
4. The trees (are our) expected to have (a an) important (affect effect) in reducing air pollution and also on global warming.
5. I wasn't (conscience conscious) before that trees can have such (a an) (affect effect) on (are our) environment.
6. (It's Its) as President Bush once said, "A tree is the oldest, cheapest, and most efficient air purifier."
7. Trees breathe in carbon dioxide, which is responsible for the greenhouse (affect effect).
8. I never (knew new) before that a single forest tree can absorb 26 pounds of carbon dioxide in a year.

9. There (<u>are</u> our) 728 million forested acres in the United States, and they remove 1.7 billion tons of carbon dioxide each year.
10. That (<u>does</u> dose) get rid of part of the 5.6 billion tons of carbon dioxide that the burning of fossil fuels releases.

JOURNAL WRITING

The surest way to learn these Words Often Confused is to use them immediately in your own writing. Therefore begin to keep a journal, writing each day at least three sentences making use of some words or rules you've learned that day. If you write about things that interest you, then you'll be inclined to reread your journal occasionally and thus review what you've learned.

WRITING ASSIGNMENT

The writing assignments, grouped together for convenience at the back of the book, are to be used along with the exercises. Turn to page 190 for your first writing assignment, or follow your instructor's directions concerning the assignments.

BEWARE

Don't assume that the Writing Section isn't important just because it's at the back of the book and has only 29 pages. IT'S THE MOST IMPORTANT PART OF THE BOOK, and you should spend more time on it than on all the rest of the book. It has been kept brief because *you learn to write by writing,* not by reading pages and pages *about* writing.

MORE WORDS OFTEN CONFUSED

Study these words carefully, with their examples, before attempting the exercises. When you've mastered all forty word groups in these two sections, you'll have taken care of many of your spelling problems.

lead, led

The past form of the verb "to lead" is *led*.
    She *led* the marching band last year.
If you don't mean past time, use *lead*, which rhymes with *bead*. (Don't confuse it with the metal *lead*, which rhymes with *dead*.)
    She will *lead* the marching band again this year.

loose, lose

Loose means "not tight." Note how *l o o s e* that word is. It has plenty of room for two *o*'s.
    My shoestring is *loose*.
The other one, *lose*, has room for only one *o*.
    We're going to *lose* the game.

moral, morale

Pronounce these two words correctly, and you won't confuse them—*móral, morále*.
Moral has to do with right and wrong.
    She has high *moral* standards.
Morale is "the spirit of a group or an individual."
    The *morale* of the team was excellent.

passed, past

The past form of the verb "to pass" is *passed*.
    He *passed* the house.
    The player *passed* the ball to her teammate.
    He *passed* his exams.
Use *past* when it's not a verb.
    He walked *past* the house. (It's the same as *He walked by the house*, so you know it isn't a verb.)
    He's coasting on his *past* reputation.
    In the *past* he had always *passed* his exams.

personal, personnel

Pronounce these two correctly, and you won't confuse them—*pérsonal, personnél*.
    He had a *personal* interest in the election.
Personnel means "a group of employees."
    She was in charge of *personnel* at the factory.

piece, peace

Remember "piece of pie." The one meaning "a *piece* of something" always begins with *pie.*

I gave him a *piece* of my mind.

The other one, *peace,* is the opposite of war.

They signed the *peace* treaty.

principal, principle

Principal means "main." Both words have *a* in them:

princip*a*l

m*a*in

The *principal* of the school spoke. (main teacher)

The *principal* problem is financial. (main problem)

He lost both *principal* and interest. (main amount of money)

A *principle* is a "rule." Both words end in *le:*

princip*le*

ru*le*

He had high moral *principles.* (rules)

That's against my *principles.* (rules)

quiet, quite

Pronounce these two correctly, and you won't confuse them. *Quiet* rhymes with *diet.*

Be *quiet.*

Quite rhymes with *bite.*

It's *quite* cold in here.

right, write

Right means "correct" or "proper."

I got ten answers *right.*

It also means in the exact location, position, or moment.

Your glasses are *right* where you left them.

Let's go *right* now.

Write is what you do with a pen.

I'm going to *write* my paper now.

than, then

Than compares two things.

I'd rather have this *than* that.

Then tells when (*then* and *when* rhyme, and both have *e* in them).

He finished his test; *then* he started home.

their, there,
they're

Their is a possessive (see pp. 32–33), meaning belonging to them.

Their house is painted pink.

There points out something. (Remember that the three words indicating a place or pointing out something all have *here* in them: *here, there, where.*)

I'm sure I left it *there*.

There were clouds in the sky.

They're is a contraction (see pp. 26–27) and means "they are."

They're happy now. (They are happy now.)

threw, through

Threw is the past form of "to throw."

He *threw* the ball.

I *threw* away my chance.

If you don't mean "to throw something," use *through*.

I walked *through* the door.

She's *through* with her work.

two, too, to

Two is a number.

I have *two* brothers.

Too means "more than enough" or "also."

The lesson was *too* difficult and *too* long. She was *too* late. (more than enough)

I found it boring *too*. (also)

I'll be at the party *too*.

Use *to* for all other meanings.

He likes *to* snorkel. He's going *to* the beach.

weather, whether

Weather refers to atmospheric conditions.

This *weather* is too hot for me.

Whether means "if."

I don't know *whether* I'll go.

Whether I'll go depends on the *weather*.

were, where

Were is the past form of the verb "to be."

We *were* miles from home.

Where refers to a place. (Remember that the three words indicating a place or pointing out something all have *here* in them: *here, there, where.*)

Where is he? There he is.

Where are you? Here I am.

who's, whose

Who's is a contraction and means "who is" or "who has."

> *Who's* there? (Who is there?)
> *Who's* been eating my pie? (Who has been . . . ?)

Whose is a possessive. (Possessives such as *whose, its, yours, hers, ours, theirs* are already possessive and never take an apostrophe. See pp. 32–33.)

> *Whose* bike is this?

woman, women

Remember that the word is just *man* or *men* with *wo* in front of it.

> wo man . . . *woman* . . . one woman
> wo men . . . *women* . . . two or more women
> That *woman* is my aunt.
> Those *women* are helping with the canvass.

you're, your

You're is a contraction and means "you are."

> *You're* very welcome. (You are very welcome.)

Your is a possessive meaning belonging to you.

> *Your* toast is ready.
> *Your* hair looks beautiful.

EXERCISES

Underline the correct word. When you've finished ten sentences, compare your answers with those at the back of the book. Do only ten sentences at a time, so you can teach yourself while you still have sentences to practice on.

☐EXERCISE 1

1. I never (knew new) that diamonds can be found (right write) (hear here) in the United States.
2. I was (conscience conscious) of (coarse course) that they (are our) found in South Africa.
3. Now, however, I've learned that (their they're) to be found in this country (too two).
4. In Crater of Diamonds State Park in Arkansas (their there) is a field of diamonds.
5. Since 1906, when the field was discovered, more (than then) seventy thousand diamonds have been found.
6. Of (coarse course) they are of little commercial value, but still (their they're) diamonds.

7. About three are found by visitors every day, and finders are keepers (too two).
8. Sometimes a visitor is lucky. I (hear here) that in 1975 one lucky searcher found a 16.37-carat diamond.
9. The field is composed of diamond-bearing earth thrust up (threw through) cracks in the earth's crust about 100 million years ago.
10. I wonder (weather whether) I'll ever get to see that field.

Source: *National Geographic Traveler,* Spring 1987

☐EXERCISE 2

1. I've been reading (a an) article about pigeon racing.
2. (It's Its) not a (knew new) sport; pigeons were raced in Palestine in the second century.
3. And (there they're) was a pigeon postal service in Baghdad in A.D. 1150.
4. Pigeons (are our) raced over mapped (coarses courses) all over the United States.
5. One of the longest races is from East Moline, Illinois, to Pawtucket, Rhode Island. (It's Its) one thousand miles.
6. Of (coarse course) (their there) is no explanation of how the pigeons find (their there) way.
7. They fly home faster (than then) their owners can drive in a car.
8. If pigeons are let (loose lose) seven hundred miles from home, they'll be home in about twelve hours, depending on the (weather whether) and (weather whether) they have a tail wind.
9. The exciting part of pigeon racing is seeing the pigeons come out of the sky at last to (their there) own loft.
10. Thirty-two pigeons got medals in World War II, including one American bird, GI Joe, which flew more (than then) a mile a minute with a message that saved the lives of hundreds of soldiers.

☐EXERCISE 3

1. (Their There) (right write) on my front lawn was a white baby rabbit.
2. Impossible! I live in the middle of the city on a (principal principle) highway that runs (threw through) the city.
3. How could a baby rabbit be (hear here) with the traffic whizzing by?
4. But (there they're) it was.
5. I opened my door softly and with (quiet quite) steps walked toward it and bent down and touched it.
6. As I began stroking (it's its) soft white fur, (it's its) nose twitched nervously.
7. (Were Where) did it come from?
8. How did it get (hear here)?

9. What could I (do due)? What agency could I call?
10. (Than Then) relief! (Their There) on the sidewalk appeared a kid from up the street. It was his pet rabbit.

☐EXERCISE 4

1. We often read about species that have become extinct (or our) that (are our) in danger of becoming extinct.
2. Now I've read about a species that supposedly had become extinct a million years ago but that now has turned up alive and well.
3. One day in 1944 a worker in China came across (a an) unusual tree beside a small stream. He collected some branches and cones and took them to a botanist.
4. The botanist found that they (were where) from the dawn redwood tree, which up until (than then) had been known only from (it's its) fossil remains.
5. The botanist sent some of the seeds to Harvard University, which (than then) distributed them widely.
6. Today dawn redwood trees (are our) flourishing around the world. A small grove of them can be seen at the National Zoological Park in Washington, D.C.
7. The dawn redwood is related to the sequoias of California although it (does dose) not grow as high.
8. It grows three feet (are or) more a year while (it's its) young, and later it reaches a height of about 150 feet.
9. Unlike other redwoods, it sheds (it's its) long green needles in the fall.
10. A few other species of plants and animals that (were where) thought in the (passed past) to be extinct (are our) now occasionally turning up.

Source: *Smithsonian,* Sept. 1990

☐EXERCISE 5

1. When fall came this year, the (weather whether) got cooler and wetter.
2. Every morning the dew made (are our) lawn glisten.
3. The (weather whether) was finally so damp that something special happened.
4. Three big white balls grew as big as golf balls (right write) in the middle of (are our) lawn.
5. I looked closely at them and saw that they (were where) mushrooms growing on thick stalks.
6. They looked like something (right write) out of a fairy tale.
7. (Than Then) I noticed even more of them growing in the shade of some bushes nearby. (There They're) were dozens of them.
8. Over the next several days I watched them unfold from a ball shape into a flat top with gills underneath.

9. (Than Then) one morning I checked, and they had all withered, victims of dryer and cooler days.
10. They (were where) like aliens who had come to visit (are our) lawn and now had returned home.

☐EXERCISE 6

1. When I think of museums I think of (coarse course) of the Field Museum in Chicago and the Smithsonian in Washington, D.C.
2. But now I (know no) (their there) are lots of museums in (are our) country that I had never heard of.
3. I've just read (a an) article describing some of them.
4. One is the Nut Museum in Old Lyme, Connecticut, (were where) (their there) is (a an) eight-foot high nutcracker and (a an) thirty-five-pound coconut, which is the largest ever grown.
5. At the Dog Museum of America in New York City (their there) (are our) replicas of Checkers and other famous White House canines.
6. In the American Museum of Fly Fishing in Manchester, Vermont, (are our) the fishing rods used by Daniel Webster, Ernest Hemingway, and Bing Crosby.
7. At the Lock Museum in Terryville, Connecticut, (are our) more (than then) twenty thousand locks, including some six-inch-long sterling silver door keys used in the (passed past) to open the gates of English castles.
8. The Uncle Remus Museum in Eatonton, Georgia, is housed in (too two) former slave cabins and honors Joel Chandler Harris and his stories about Br'er Rabbit.
9. In the Hall of Flame in Phoenix (there they're) (are our) thousands of firemen's uniforms in addition to restored vehicles dating back to 1725.
10. In the Grocery Hall of Fame in Vancouver, British Columbia, it seems as if (you're your) in a corner store of fifty years ago with more (than then) ten thousand products on display.

☐EXERCISE 7

1. I never (knew new) before that any bird was smaller (than then) the hummingbirds that come to (are our) backyard each summer.
2. Now I've read (a an) article about the smallest bird in the world; (it's its) the bee hummingbird of Cuba.
3. (It's Its) only a bit more (than then) two inches long from beak to tail. Only the male is the smallest bird, however, because the female is about a quarter of (a an) inch longer.
4. The male bee hummingbird weighs about two grams, which is less (than then) the weight of a penny.

5. (It's Its) wings beat eighty times per second—so fast that the human eye can't see the wings and often mistakes the bird for a buzzing insect.
6. The bee hummingbird doesn't live anywhere (accept except) Cuba, and there is lives only in the most inaccessible regions.
7. The birds (are our) loners and bond with the other sex only for the few seconds it takes to mate.
8. Once they were widespread across Cuba, but (all ready already) they (are our) thought to be (a an) endangered species.
9. Despite Cuba's conservation efforts, the birds (are our) now seen only rarely in (their there) dwindling habitat.
10. Of (coarse course) reading about such birds (does dose) make one (conscience conscious) of how important the tropical forests are.

Source: *National Geographic,* June 1990

☐EXERCISE 8

1. I've been reading (a an) article about Anchorage, Alaska, and I've learned some things I never (knew new) before.
2. (It's Its) winter weather is milder (than then) I'd (have of) expected.
3. The temperature is around 20°F most of the winter, but the days (are our) short and the nights long.
4. In the summer, however, the sun sets only briefly, and the days (are or) so long that Midnight Sun Baseball is played.
5. (There They're) is also the Midnight Sun Hot Balloon Classic, which is (a an) airborne race that fills the sky with dozens of bright balloons.
6. With twenty hours of sunlight each day in the summer, vegetables grow to (quiet quite) amazing sizes.
7. At the Alaska State Fair, (were where) the vegetables are exhibited, (it's its) common to see seven-pound turnips and seventy-pound cabbages.
8. Anchorage is (a an) amazing city with old wooden houses from the (passed past) standing beside fifteen-story hotels, and of (coarse course) glaciers and black bears are not far away.
9. Nearby (there they're) are 125 miles of splendid bicycle paths, which in the winter become cross-country ski trails.
10. I (do due) want to go (their there) sometime.

☐EXERCISE 9

1. I don't (know no) (weather whether) I'm going to remember all these words.
2. My (principal principle) difficulty in this (coarse course) (does dose) seem to be spelling.

3. (It's Its) no wonder we all have problems with spelling because (are our) English language is so difficult to (right write).
4. Over 80 percent of (are our) words aren't spelled phonetically.
5. For example, the *ow* in *crow* sounds (quiet quite) different from the *ow* in *cow.*
6. A sound may be spelled in four (are or) five different ways.
7. Since taking this (coarse course), I spell better (than then) before.
8. I now (know no) most of these often-confused words.
9. Even if I forget them, I (know no) (were where) to look them up.
10. I'm (quiet quite) sure I'm making progress, and I'll learn more before I'm (threw through).

□EXERCISE 10

1. (Are Our) geography class took (a an) interesting field trip to Crater Lake last fall.
2. (There They're) is (know no) more beautiful spot in all Oregon.
3. The lake is (quiet quite) and peaceful, but (it's its) origin wasn't peaceful.
4. In the (passed past) the spot (were where) the lake now lies was a huge volcano.
5. First the volcano erupted; (than then) (it's its) top caved in and left the huge crater.
6. Since (their there) is no inlet or outlet to the crater, water from rain and snow has accumulated (threw through) the years.
7. It must (have of) taken a long time for the tremendous pit to (feel fill) with water.
8. I (know no) (it's its) the deepest lake in the United States and the seventh deepest in the world.
9. (It's Its) unusual beauty is in (it's its) sapphire blue water, which is bluer (than then) any other lake water I've seen.
10. In the middle of the lake is a small cinder cone, Wizard Island, which I (hear here) was made by (quiet quite) a late volcano eruption only one thousand years ago.

JOURNAL WRITING

In your journal write several sentences using any words you missed in doing the exercises.

Journal writing is a good idea not only because it will help you remember these words often confused but also because it will be a storehouse for ideas you can later use in writing papers. Here are some ideas you might consider writing your sentences about:

—Your goals
—Your thoughts about a class discussion
—A new idea you've gained from a course
—Your reaction to a movie or play
—An experience that has made you think
—What you've learned from a friendship
—How you're working through a problem
—How your values are changing

WRITING ASSIGNMENT

From now on, along with doing the exercises, you will be expected to follow your instructor's directions concerning the writing assignments, which begin on page 188.

Proofreading Exercise

See if you can correct the six errors in this student paragraph.

THE ALARM CLOCK

When I was a freshman in high school, I took apart a old windup alarm clock that wouldn't run. I new I could fix it. Their sure are a lot of wheels and levers and gears and things in an alarm clock, but they all fit together beautifully. I could see how they all worked, but when I started to put the parts back were they logically belonged, I couldn't remember the exact pattern. When I was all threw, I had two gears left over. And of coarse the clock didn't work. However, the day was worthwhile because I learned a lot about windup alarm clocks. I learned not to take one apart unless I'm positive I can put it back together!

USE OF APOSTROPHE: CONTRACTIONS

Two words condensed into one is called a contraction:

is not→isn't   you have→you've

The letter or letters that are left out are replaced with an apostrophe. For example, if the two words *do not* are condensed into one, an apostrophe is put where the *o* is left out.

do not   don't

Note how the apostrophe goes in the exact place where the letter or letters are left out in these contractions:

I am	I'm
I have	I've
I shall, I will	I'll
I would	I'd
you are	you're
you have	you've
you will	you'll
she is, she has	she's
he is, he has	he's
it is, it has	it's
we are	we're
we have	we've
we will, we shall	we'll
they are	they're
they have	they've
are not	aren't
cannot	can't
do not	don't
does not	doesn't
have not	haven't
let us	let's
who is, who has	who's
where is	where's
were not	weren't
would not	wouldn't
could not	couldn't
should not	shouldn't
would have	would've
could have	could've

should have	should've
that is	that's
there is	there's
what is	what's

One contraction does not follow this rule: *will not* becomes *won't*.

In all other contractions that you're likely to use, the apostrophe goes exactly where the letter or letters are left out. Note especially *it's*, *they're*, *who's*, and *you're*. Use them when you mean two words. (See pp. 26–27 for the possessive forms—*its*, *their*, *whose*, and *your*—which don't take an apostrophe.)

EXERCISES

Put an apostrophe in each contraction. Then compare your answers with those at the back of the book. Be sure to correct each group of ten sentences before going on so you'll catch your mistakes while you still have sentences to practice on.

☐EXERCISE 1

1. Ive been reading that scientists are studying noise levels.
2. Theyre looking for ways to reduce noise levels near airports and other places where noise cant be eliminated.
3. Theyve found that one way to muffle sound is to plant small forests.
4. The forest floor with its heavy layer of decaying leaves absorbs sound like a sponge.
5. Also its been found that tree trunks deflect sound to the forest floor.
6. Forests not only muffle sound; theyre also useful as visual screens.
7. If people cant see where sound comes from, they arent so disturbed by it.
8. Thus city planners find its worthwhile to plant small urban forests.
9. But the forests arent only sound barriers.
10. Theyre pleasant recreation spots as well.

☐EXERCISE 2

1. I didnt know that there havent always been drinking straws.
2. Ive always just taken straws for granted.
3. Now Ive learned that before 1888—just a little more than a hundred years ago—there werent any straws.
4. In fact straws hadnt even been thought of.
5. People drank their soda or lemonade through the hollow stalks of rye grain.

6. It wasn't an easy way to drink.
7. The rye stalks were often cracked, and they weren't exactly clean.
8. Then in 1888 someone took out a patent for making drinking straws out of paraffin-coated manila paper.
9. It didn't take long for those straws to catch on.
10. Consuming cool drinks on hot afternoons hasn't been the same since.

Source: *American Heritage,* Feb. 1988

□EXERCISE 3

1. Haven't you noticed how many people are riding bicycles these days?
2. I've just read that bicycles recently outsold cars for the first time in many years.
3. Today bicycles aren't merely for diversion; they're an important means of transportation.
4. And they aren't only energy savers; they're health builders as well.
5. There's nothing better for the cardiovascular system than a bicycle ride.
6. If you've had a bicycle ride in the morning, you'll feel better all day.
7. Some cities are aware of the trend; they're putting in bicycle lanes.
8. It's a problem, though, to make room for bicycles on busy city streets.
9. It's going to take time to solve the conflict between bicycles and cars.
10. But bicycles save fuel, provide healthful exercise, and leave the air clean; they're not to be taken lightly.

□EXERCISE 4

1. I've just come back from EPCOT, and I can't begin to describe all that's there.
2. There's so much that I didn't begin to see it all.
3. I'll never forget my amazement at the exhibits of nine countries in the World Showcase.
4. It's exciting to "ride a buckboard" at the Calgary Stampede.
5. I'd never before seen a Japanese house or a Mexican hacienda.
6. It's fascinating to go to the end of the Great Wall in China and to a pub in England.
7. Then there's Future World, in which I flew aboard a space vehicle.
8. You'll learn a lot if you visit EPCOT, and you'll want to stay awhile.
9. It's an education to go there, and I'm planning to go back.
10. Also I'm now planning to see the originals of some of those exhibits.

□EXERCISE 5

1. I'm doing more reading now, and I find it's helping my writing.
2. I'd never before realized that it's important to read widely.

3. Ive begun to notice good sentences and how theyre put together.
4. Also, just by reading Ive improved my vocabulary.
5. Im beginning to look up words I dont know.
6. Its amazing how many new words Ive already learned.
7. Ive found that reading has helped my spelling too.
8. Im getting used to seeing words spelled correctly, and Im automatically spelling better.
9. Its good also to know whats in the books people are talking about.
10. Ive found that reading can do a lot for me that TV cant.

□EXERCISE 6

1. Theres nothing quite like the thrill that comes when you know youve made a good goal in hockey.
2. Maybe you werent the one who shot the puck into the net, but if you assisted, you were part of making the goal.
3. Every player whos assisted in that goal gets a thrill.
4. Anyone who knows the sport knows that scoring is a team effort with several players contributing to each goal.
5. Now that Im out in the business world, Ive discovered that business is just like hockey.
6. Everyone who works on a project gets a thrill when its goal is reached.
7. The one who sets up the project isnt the only one whos responsible.
8. Everyone whos part of the project helps make that goal.
9. Its a team effort just like hockey.
10. When Im on the team, I get a thrill just the way I used to when I helped make a perfect goal in hockey.

□EXERCISE 7

1. Ive been reading about some famous people who didnt do well in school.
2. Its made me feel better.
3. Woody Allen says he didnt get any awards in school, and his grades "varied from below average to way below average."
4. I hadnt known before that Einstein failed his entrance exams at the Zurich Polytechnical Institute.
5. Louis Pasteur didnt fail, but the word *mediocre* was written after *Chemistry* on his diploma.
6. Winston Churchill didnt do well in school and says he stayed in the lowest grades three times longer than anyone else.
7. Charles Schulz, the cartoonist who created Charlie Brown, not only wasnt good in school but didnt even succeed at first with his cartoons.

8. Its a fact that his high school yearbook wouldnt accept them.
9. Perhaps grades arent the most important thing.
10. Hey, with my grades, maybe Ill become famous!

☐EXERCISE 8

1. Ive just read an article about bats.
2. And Ive learned some things I never knew before.
3. Id always disliked bats because I thought they were ugly and dirty.
4. But now Ive learned that theyre the victims of prejudice and misinformation.
5. Actually theyre well-organized, intelligent, and beneficial.
6. Theyre beneficial because they pollinate banana plants, figs, dates, and cashews.
7. Also theyre always eating insects.
8. Each night they consume more than one-third of their body weight eating flying ants, beetles, and moths.
9. A bat can chase insects through a dark forest and wont ever strike a branch or a twig.
10. Many bats have poor eyesight.

☐EXERCISE 9

1. But its not its eyes but its ears that guide a bat.
2. The sound waves of its cry are reflected back to its sensitive ears.
3. Thus it doesnt hit any obstacles.
4. The kinds of insects that bats consume cost farmers and foresters millions of dollars annually.
5. Thus the bats are of ecological importance.
6. In North America its the little brown bat thats most abundant.
7. Its 3½ inches long and weighs only half an ounce.
8. A single little brown bat can catch 500 mosquito-size insects in an hour.
9. Bats are mammals, and theyre the only mammals that fly.
10. To start flying, a bat drops from its perch.

☐EXERCISE 10

1. If its on the ground, it crawls to some height where its possible to drop into the air.
2. There are more than 900 species of bats.
3. One bat in the Malay Peninsula has a wingspan of sixty inches.
4. Its the largest bat.
5. The smallest bat is only one inch long.
6. A bat cant walk or run.

7. Its legs and feet arent strong enough to do anything but hold onto a perch when its time to sleep.
8. The female brown bat doesnt have a nest.
9. But she gives birth to a single pink blind baby each year.
10. When shes ready to go away for food, she simply hangs the baby up by its feet.

JOURNAL WRITING

Doing exercises helps you learn a rule, but even more helpful is using the rule in writing. In your journal write some sentences using contractions. You might write about your reaction to the week's news. Or choose your own subject.

WRITING ASSIGNMENT

Turn to the writing section at the back of the book for your writing assignment.

Proofreading Exercise

Can you correct the five errors in this paragraph? No answers are provided.

I always have a hard time starting to study. I do everything accept face
my books. Often I turn on my computer and start playing a adventure
game. Its fun, but of coarse I get more and more behind in my studies. I
just wish I new how to turn my brain onto studying mode.

USE OF APOSTROPHE: POSSESSIVES

The trick in writing possessives is to ask yourself the question, "Who (or what) does it belong to?" (Modern usage has made *who* acceptable when it comes first in a sentence, but some people still say, "*Whom* does it belong to?" or even "*To whom* does it belong?") If the answer to your question ends in *s*, simply add an apostrophe. If it doesn't end in *s*, then add an apostrophe and *s*.

one boys bike	Who does it belong to?	boy	Add *'s*	boy's bike
two boys bikes	Who do they belong to?	boys	Add *'*	boys' bikes
the mans hat	Who does it belong to?	man	Add *'s*	man's hat
the mens hats	Who do they belong to?	men	Add *'s*	men's hats
childrens game	Who does it belong to?	children	Add *'s*	children's game
a days work	What does it belong to?	day	Add *'s*	day's work
Carlos roommate	Who does he belong to?	Carlos	Add *'*	Carlos' roommate

This trick will always work, but you must ask the question every time. Remember that the key word is *belong*. Who (or what) does it belong to? If you ask the question another way, you may get an answer that won't help you. Also, if you just look at a word without asking the question, you may think the name of the owner ends in *s* when it really doesn't.

TO MAKE A POSSESSIVE

Ask "Who (or what) does it belong to?"
If the answer ends in *s*, just add an apostrophe.
If it doesn't end in *s*, add an apostrophe and *s*.

Cover the right-hand column and see if you can write the following possessives correctly. Ask the question each time.

the womans dress ————————————————— woman's

the womens ideas ————————————————— women's

Kathys room ————————————————— Kathy's

James room ————————————————— James'

the Jacksons house ————————————————— the Jacksons'

Mr. Jacksons house ————————————————— Mr. Jackson's

Jonas book ————————————————— Jonas'

the ladys house ————————————————— lady's

the ladies meeting ————————————————— ladies'

(Sometimes you may see a variation of this rule. *James' book* may be written *James's book*. That is correct too, but the best way is to stick to the simple rule. You can't be wrong if you follow it.)

A word of warning! Don't assume that because a word ends in *s* it is necessarily a possessive. It may indicate more than one of something. Make sure the word actually possesses something before you add an apostrophe.

A few words are already possessive and don't need an apostrophe added to them. Memorize this list:

my, mine	its
your, yours	our, ours
his	their, theirs
her, hers	whose

Note particularly *its, their, whose,* and *your.* They are already possessive and don't take an apostrophe. (They sound just like the contractions *it's, they're, who's,* and *you're,* which stand for two words and of course have to have an apostrophe.)

As a practice exercise, cover the right-hand column below with a sheet of paper, and on it write the correct form (contraction or possessive). If you miss any, go back and review the explanations.

(It) snowing. —————————————— It's

(You) car needs washing. —————————————— Your

(Who) heading the committee? —————————————— Who's

(They) planning to go. —————————————— They're

The cat ate (it) food. —————————————— its

(Who) fault was it? —————————————— Whose

The wind lost (it) force. —————————————— its

(Who) responsible? —————————————— Who's

(They) buying a minivan. —————————————— They're

(It) all I can do. —————————————— It's

(You) excused. —————————————— You're

(They) house has six rooms. —————————————— Their

(You) in the lead. —————————————— You're

(Who) car shall we take? —————————————— Whose

I like (you) color scheme. —————————————— your

Here's one more practice exercise. Cover the right-hand column with a sheet of paper, and on it write the possessives.

1. My cousins love their Aunt Anns house.	Ann's (You didn't add an apostrophe to *cousins,* did you? The cousins don't possess anything.)
2. Students grades depend on their study habits.	Students' (Who do the grades belong to?)
3. I invited Charles to my parents house.	parents' (Charles doesn't possess anything in this sentence.)
4. Two of my friends went to Charles graduation.	Charles' (The friends don't possess anything in this sentence.)
5. Robins job is similar to yours.	Robin's (*Yours* is already possessive and doesn't take an apostrophe.)
6. Last years crop was the best yet.	year's (The crop belonged to last year.)
7. The Fowlers cottage is near the lake.	Fowlers' (Who does the cottage belong to?)
8. The Fowlers went to their cottage.	(No apostrophe in this sentence. The sentence merely tells what the Fowlers did.)
9. The womens team played the girls team.	women's, girls' (Did you ask who each team belongs to?)
10. The girls were proud of their team.	(No apostrophe. *Their* is already possessive, and the girls don't possess anything in this sentence.)
11. The jurors gave their verdict.	(No apostrophe. The sentence merely tells what the jurors did.)
12. The jurors verdict was fair.	jurors' (Who did the verdict belong to?)
13. Les borrowed someone elses book.	someone else's (Who did the book belong to?)
14. The sign by the gate said "The Buxtons."	Buxtons (meaning that the Buxtons live there) or Buxtons' (meaning that it's the Buxtons' house)
15. We went to last nights game.	night's (The game belonged to last night.)

EXERCISES

Put the apostrophe in each possessive. WATCH OUT! **First,** make sure the word really possesses something; not every word ending in *s* is a possessive. **Second,** remember that certain words are already possessive and don't take an apostrophe. **Third,** remember that even though a word ends in *s,* you can't tell where the apostrophe goes until you ask the question, "Who (or what) does it belong to?" In the first sentence, for example, "Who does the watch belong to?" "Man." Therefore you'll write *man's.*

□EXERCISE 1

1. Here's a mans watch on the table.
2. Whose book is that on the floor?
3. It may be either Kimberlys or Sarahs.
4. Have you seen Alfredos guitar?
5. Perhaps he left it in its case at the student union.
6. Everyones possessions seem to be lost today.
7. Yesterday my sister Bess car keys were lost.
8. She finally had to borrow my dads car.
9. Then somebodys car was parked in front of our driveway, and she couldn't get out.
10. Therefore she missed seeing yesterdays game.

□EXERCISE 2

1. Today our instructor read everybodys paper in class.
2. The students comments about the papers were interesting.
3. One persons paper had excellent specific details.
4. Someone elses paper was amusing.
5. Someones paper showed a lot of research.
6. Two students papers were exceptionally well organized.
7. All the students comments were helpful to the writers.
8. Our instructors suggestions were also valuable.
9. All except one students paper will now be rewritten.
10. Everybodys paper is sure to be improved.

□EXERCISE 3

1. I've decided to buy some gifts at Saturdays sale.
2. Then I'll have them ready for everybodys birthday.
3. I'm going to look at mens ties and womens scarves.
4. That store sells only boys and mens clothing.
5. Of course I'll look at childrens toys for my nephews.
6. Perhaps I can find a book for my nieces gift.
7. Jewelry is always a safe choice for my sisters gift.

8. My parents gift will probably be a video for their VCR.
9. It looks as if I'll have a mornings work buying all these things.
10. But I enjoy choosing gifts for peoples birthdays.

□EXERCISE 4

1. I went to the local Womens Club yesterday because I wanted to hear the state senator speak.
2. The club presidents introduction of the senator was good.
3. All the women enjoyed their presidents jokes.
4. Then the senators speech was interesting and informative.
5. She explained the Senates problems clearly.
6. Then she answered the womens questions.
7. At the end the womens applause was tremendous.
8. Without doubt the women who heard her will give her their votes.
9. But who will win the fall election is anyones guess.
10. At least I'm glad I heard the senators presentation.

□EXERCISE 5

1. Last summers job was very important to me.
2. I made enough money for an entire years tuition.
3. But even more important was each days experience.
4. I never thought being a bagger at Bens Grocery would teach me anything, but it did.
5. First of all, I learned that the customers request is important.
6. Then I learned how silly some customers requests can be.
7. One womans insistence on a different bag for each kind of food was absurd.
8. But the managers orders were to satisfy the customer.
9. Finally I learned how to keep smiling even at the days end.
10. And most important, I learned to remember a baggers feelings.

□EXERCISE 6

1. A visitors first impression of the Science Museum of Minnesota in St. Paul will be surprise.
2. Here are exhibits that people can touch, try out, and experiment with.
3. Peoples approval of the museum is shown by the ten thousand visitors each week.
4. Childrens voices are heard asking questions, and people are interacting with the exhibits.
5. The four hundred volunteer interpreters answer all the visitors questions.
6. Visitors can help set up and take down an Ojibwa Indian wigwam and touch the Indians pots and bows and arrows.

7. Sitting at a loom and weaving a strand of wool in and out of the warp should satisfy anyones curiosity about weaving.
8. On the second floor is the countrys most advanced space theater.
9. A persons first impression of the space theater is that its semicircular dome and rounded walls wrap right around the audience.
10. Then in a film on the Great Barrier Reef, the viewer seems to be swimming among the fish and sharks and marine plant life.

☐EXERCISE 7

1. Sallys chief interest is butterflies, and she's been telling me about them.
2. Butterflies are everywhere—from the equator to the poles.
3. There are twenty thousand named species of butterflies.
4. Butterflies wingspans range from a quarter of an inch to ten inches.
5. Butterflies bodies are divided into three sections: each section has a pair of legs, and the middle section also has two pairs of wings.
6. A butterflys mouth is a long, slender feeding tube that is coiled up when not in use.
7. Birds are the butterflies main enemies, but some butterflies mottled colors enable them to blend in with their surroundings and thus escape the birds.
8. The prominent eyespots on some butterflies wings startle the birds, which mistake the spots for rodents eyes or snakes eyes.
9. If the butterfly flaps its wings and thus makes the "eyes" blink, the resemblance is even stronger.
10. The monarch butterflys foul taste and odor give it an even better defense against the birds.

☐EXERCISE 8

1. On last summers trip across the Midwest, we stopped in Salt Lake City.
2. It's Utahs largest and most important city.
3. My moms first comment was about the cleanliness of the city.
4. No broken bottles or discarded plastic containers mar the city streets.
5. Moms second comment was about the quiet atmosphere—quite unlike that of the cities we had come through elsewhere.
6. Our familys main interest was in Temple Square, which contains the Mormon Temple, the Tabernacle, and ten acres of beautiful gardens.
7. Everybodys attention was captured when a guide, demonstrating the famous acoustics of the Tabernacle, dropped a pin, and we heard the sound 170 feet away.
8. My dads interest was in the famed organ recital at noon.

9. In the evening we heard the nearly four hundred voices of the Tabernacle Choir.
10. We wished we could have stayed long enough to trace our ancestry in the worlds largest genealogical library.

☐EXERCISE 9

1. Everybodys interest in physical fitness has increased lately.
2. The advice of the medical profession about exercise preventing disease has had a great effect.
3. One persons activity spurs another person on.
4. Now all my friends are exercise buffs, but each persons interest is different.
5. Kents interest is in jogging whereas his brothers is in working out with weights.
6. Amandas devotion is to ballet, and her sisters is to ice-skating.
7. Several of my friends enjoy a days skiing.
8. Some of them spend an entire weeks vacation on water sports.
9. As for me, an evenings work in my garden suffices.
10. Everyones taste differs, but we're all getting our exercise.

☐EXERCISE 10

1. I have been reading about a persons greatest danger in life.
2. A persons greatest danger is not from lions or tigers or rattlesnakes.
3. The greatest danger is from a creature right on your breakfast table.
4. That creatures name is the common housefly.
5. A housefly can carry as many as six million disease-carrying bacteria on its body.
6. The germs ride on the flys hairy body and sticky footpads.
7. Flyborne diseases include cholera, tuberculosis, polio, and many eye diseases.
8. So swat that fly if you want to avoid the flys diseases.
9. Mosquitoes stings are more deadly still because they carry the viruses of malaria and yellow fever.
10. Worldwide they cause some 300 million peoples illnesses each year.

JOURNAL WRITING

In your journal write some sentences using the possessive forms of the names of members of your family or the names of your friends.

WRITING ASSIGNMENT

As you continue with the exercises, continue also with the writing assignments in the latter part of the book.

Review of Contractions and Possessives

Add the necessary apostrophes. Try to get these exercises perfect. Don't excuse an error by saying, "Oh, that was just a careless mistake." A mistake is a mistake. Be tough on yourself.

☐EXERCISE 1

1. Ive been reading about how bananas grow.
2. Id always though they grew on trees, but they dont.
3. A banana plants stalk isnt like the trunk of a tree; its stalk is made of overlapping leaves like those of a celery stalk.
4. When the stalk is full grown, its from eight to sixteen inches thick but so soft it can be cut with a knife.
5. A banana plants leaves may be twelve feet long and more than two feet wide.
6. In some countries the leaves are torn into strips to make mats, and the fibers are used to make twine.
7. When the blossoms of a banana plant fall off, a cluster of tiny bananas pointing toward the ground can be seen.
8. Thats the way Id always thought bananas grew, but they dont.
9. As they grow they begin to point upward, and when theyre fully grown, theyre all pointing toward the sky.
10. Then theyre harvested and may travel as much as four thousand miles to our grocery stores.

☐EXERCISE 2

1. Ive just been to a planetarium, and Ive learned some things about the solar system.
2. For instance, your bodys weight would be different on the sun and the planets from what it is here on Earth.
3. If you went to Jupiter, for example, you couldnt land because theres no solid surface.
4. But its such a huge planet that its pull of gravity is two and a half times greater than the pull of gravity here on Earth.
5. If you could land, and if you weigh 119 pounds here on Earth, your weight on Jupiter would be about 298 pounds.
6. If you were transported to the sun, youd find it a boiling ball of hot gasses with a temperature of about 10,000° F.
7. You couldnt land, of course, but if you could, the sun contains so much matter that its gravity is enormous, and youd weigh about 3,264 pounds.
8. A planets size influences its gravity pull, and on the small planet Mars youd weigh only 48 pounds.

9. And on the moon, gravitys pull is so small that youd weigh only 19 pounds.
10. Theres nothing like a visit to a planetarium to acquaint you with the solar system.

Proofreading Exercise

Can you correct the four errors in this paragraph about travel in Canada? No answers are provided.

GOING METRIC

Last summer I drove threw a part of Canada and was shocked to find the speed limit marked 100. Then I noticed that this was in kilometers per hour, which made it about the same as the American speed limit. Than I saw the temperature listed as 22 degrees, which sounded pretty cold to me. But then I realized that Canadians use the centigrade scale for temperature. So actually it was a nice day. Its hard to get used to these changes when you've been in the U.S. all you're life, but soon I was fairly familiar with them. Food is sold by the kilogram and liquids by the liter. By the end of my trip I found that the Canadian way is simpler than trying to remember how many feet are in a mile and how many ounces in a pound. So by the time I got back to the U.S. I was almost converted.

WORDS THAT CAN BE BROKEN INTO PARTS

Breaking words into their parts will often help you spell them correctly. Each of the following words is made up of two shorter words. Note that the word then contains all the letters of the two shorter words.

book keeper	... bookkeeper		room mate	... roommate
over run	... overrun		tail light	... taillight
over rate	... overrate		with hold	... withhold

Becoming aware of prefixes such as *dis, inter, mis,* and *un* is also helpful. When you add a prefix to a word, note that no letters are dropped, either from the prefix or from the word.

dis appear	disappear	mis informed	misinformed
dis appoint	disappoint	mis spell	misspell
dis approve	disapprove	mis step	misstep
dis satisfied	dissatisfied	un aware	unaware
dis service	disservice	un natural	unnatural
inter act	interact	un necessary	unnecessary
inter racial	interracial	un nerve	unnerve
inter related	interrelated	un noticed	unnoticed

Have someone dictate the above list for you to write and then mark any words you miss. Memorize the correct spellings by noting how each word is made up of a prefix and a word.

RULE FOR DOUBLING A FINAL CONSONANT

Most spelling rules have so many exceptions that they aren't much help. But here's one that has almost no exceptions and is worth learning.

Double a final consonant when adding an ending that begins with a vowel (such as *ing, ed, er*) if all three of the following are true:

1. **the word ends in a single consonant,**
2. **which is preceded by a single vowel (the vowels are *a, e, i, o, u*),**
3. **and the accent is on the last syllable (or the word has only one syllable).**

We'll try the rule on a few words to which we'll add *ing, ed,* or *er.*

begin
1. It ends in a single consonant—*n,*
2. preceded by a single vowel—*i,*
3. and the accent is on the last syllable—*be gin'.*

Therefore we double the final consonant and write *begin-ning, beginner.*

stop
1. It ends in a single consonant—*p,*
2. preceded by a single vowel—*o,*
3. and the accent is on the last syllable (there is only one).

Therefore we double the final consonant and write *stopping, stopped, stopper.*

motor
1. It ends in a single consonant—*r,*
2. preceded by a single vowel—*o,*
3. But the accent isn't on the last syllable. It's on the first—*mo'tor.*

Therefore we don't double the final consonant. We write *motoring, motored.*

sleep
1. It ends in a single consonant—*p,*
2. but it isn't preceded by a single vowel. There are two *e*'s.

Therefore we don't double the final consonant. We write *sleeping, sleeper.*

Note that *qu* is treated as a consonant because *q* is almost never written without *u.* Think of it as *kw.* In words like *equip* and *quit,* the *qu* acts as a consonant. Therefore *quit* does not end in a single consonant preceded by a single vowel, and the final consonant is doubled—*quitting.*

Also note that *bus* may be written either *bussing* or *busing.* The latter, contrary to our rule, is more common.

EXERCISES

Add *ing* to these words. Correct each group of ten before continuing so you'll catch any errors while you still have words to practice on.

□EXERCISE 1

1. drop
2. droop
3. compel
4. mop
5. plan
6. hop
7. begin
8. knit
9. mark
10. creep

□EXERCISE 2

1. offer
2. brag
3. honor
4. benefit
5. loaf
6. nail
7. omit
8. occur
9. shop
10. interrupt

□EXERCISE 3

1. refer
2. happen
3. submit
4. interpret
5. prefer
6. excel
7. wrap
8. stop
9. wed
10. scream

□EXERCISE 4

1. abandon
2. differ
3. confer
4. weed
5. subtract
6. stream
7. expel
8. miss
9. get
10. stress

□EXERCISE 5

1. hinder
2. prohibit
3. war
4. suffer
5. pin
6. trust
7. sip
8. flop
9. reap
10. cart

Progress Test

This test covers everything you've studied so far. One sentence in each pair is correct. The other is incorrect. Read both sentences carefully before you decide. Then write the letter of the correct sentence in the blank.

_____ 1. A. The Graham's cottage has just been painted.
       B. My dad's principal hobby is fishing.

_____ 2. A. It doesn't matter whether she comes or not.
       B. Her coming won't have any effect on my plans.

_____ 3. A. I'm going to chose my clothes with care this fall.
       B. The Ransoms have invited us to their barbecue.

_____ 4. A. I know it's important to cut out desserts.
       B. But he past me a piece of cake, and I took it.

_____ 5. A. He submited his application for the job.
       B. I wonder whether I should apply too.

_____ 6. A. Is this passbook yours or hers?
       B. She's quiet sure she won't lose any money.

_____ 7. A. Of coarse I know you're doing all your exercises.
       B. I omitted the fourth sentence in our test.

_____ 8. A. I've all ready saved quite a large sum of money.
       B. I'd like to save an even greater sum than that.

_____ 9. A. She wasn't conscious that he hadn't voted.
       B. She should of asked him for his personal opinion.

_____ 10. A. It's an honor to know the principal of the Academy.
       B. I like belonging to the mens' athletic club.

_____ 11. A. Our puppy got loose from it's leash and ran away.
       B. I already knew what they wanted to hear.

_____ 12. A. Your going to their beach party, aren't you?
       B. I'm not sure whether it's too rainy to go.

_____ 13. A. Who's car is that in the Millers' driveway?
       B. Won't they be through with their new project soon?

_____ 14. A. If I ever lose my keys, I won't know where to look for them.
       B. Of course Debbies advice surprised me.

_____ 15. A. He lead his class in math and got a compliment from the prof.
       B. Now he's studying harder than ever before.

USING YOUR DICTIONARY

By working through the following thirteen exercises, you'll become familiar with what you can find in an up-to-date desk dictionary.

1. PRONUNCIATION

Look up the word *mischievous* and copy the pronunciation here.

Now under each letter with a pronunciation mark over it, write the key word having the same mark. You'll find the key words at the bottom of one of the two dictionary pages open before you. Note especially that the upside-down *e* (ə) always has the sound of *uh* like the *a* in *ago* or *about*. Remember that sound because it's found in many words.

Next, pronounce the key words you have written, and then slowly pronounce *mischievous*, giving each syllable the same sound as its key word.

Finally note which syllable has the heavy accent mark. (In most dictionaries the accent mark points to the stressed syllable, but in one dictionary it is in front of the stressed syllable.) The stressed syllable is *mis*. Now say the word, letting the full force of your voice fall on that syllable.

When more than one pronunciation is given, the first is more common. If the complete pronunciation of a word isn't given, look at the word above it to find the pronunciation.

Look up the pronunciation of these words, using the key words at the bottom of the dictionary page to help you pronounce each syllable. Then note which syllable has the heavy accent mark, and say the word aloud.

condolence   comparable   koala   longevity

2. DEFINITIONS

The dictionary may give more than one meaning for a word. Read all the meanings for each italicized word and then write a definition appropriate to the sentence.

1. She felt *apathetic* about her new job. _____

   _____

2. His *sedentary* occupation gave him no opportunity to exercise. _____

   _____

3. He felt *ambivalent* about staying in college for another year. _____

   _____

4. The orchestra conductor always maintained his *equanimity* even

   under the most trying circumstances. _____

   _____

3. SPELLING

By making yourself look up each word you aren't sure how to spell, you'll soon become a better speller. When two spellings are given in the dictionary, the first one (or the one with the definition) is the more common.

Underline the more common spelling of each of these words.

ax, axe   dialog, dialogue

archaeology, archeology   gray, grey

4. COMPOUND WORDS

If you want to find out whether two words are written separately, written with a hyphen between them, or written as one word, consult your dictionary. For example:

> half sister   is written as two words
> brother-in-law   is hyphenated
> stepson   is written as one word

Write each of the following correctly:

non conformity _____   two thirds _____

runner up _____   week end _____

5. CAPITALIZATION

If a word is capitalized in the dictionary, that means it should always be capitalized. If it is not capitalized in the dictionary, then it may or may not be capitalized, depending on how it is used (see p. 174). For example:

> Indian   is always capitalized
> college   is capitalized or not, according to how it is used
>   She's attending college.
>   She's attending Community College of Philadelphia.

Write these words as they're given in the dictionary (with or without a capital) to show whether they must always be capitalized or not.

Chickadee _____   Halloween _____

Democrat _____   Spanish _____

6. USAGE

Just because a word is in the dictionary doesn't mean that it's in standard use. The following labels indicate whether a word is used today and, if so, where and by whom.

obsolete	no longer used
archaic	not now used in ordinary language but still found in some biblical, literary, and legal expressions
colloquial ⎫ informal ⎭	used in informal conversation but not in formal writing
dialectal ⎫ regional ⎭	used in some localities but not everywhere
slang	popular but nonstandard expression
nonstandard ⎫ substandard ⎭	not used by educated people

Look up each italicized word and write the label indicating its usage. Dictionaries differ. One may list a word as slang whereas another will call it colloquial. Still another may give no designation, thus indicating that that particular dictionary considers the word in standard use.

1. He's *uptight* about the new regulations. _____

2. We have a new *prof* in English. _____

3. I *goofed* on that third exam question. _____

4. Add just a *smidgen* of salt to the recipe. _____

5. We were told not to go but went *anyways*. _____

7. DERIVATIONS

The derivations or stories behind words will often help you remember the current meanings. For example, if you read that someone has a laconic style and you consult your dictionary, you'll find that *laconic* comes from the ancient province of Laconia in Greece. The Laconians were so well known for their concise way of speaking that *laconic* came to mean "brief and pithy." The story is told that Philip of Macedon, at war with the Laconians, sent word to them that if he came within their borders, he would not leave one stone standing in their capital city, Sparta. The Laconians sent back the laconic reply, "If." And so today anyone who writes or speaks briefly and to the point is said to have a laconic style.

Look up the derivation of each of these words. You'll find it in square brackets either just before or just after the definition.

aster _____

metropolis _____

tantalize _____

sandwich _____

8. SYNONYMS

At the end of a definition, a group of synonyms is sometimes given. For example, at the end of the definition of *beautiful*, you'll find several synonyms. And if you look up *handsome* or *pretty*, you'll be referred to the synonyms under *beautiful*.

List the synonyms for the following words.

new _____

acknowledge _____

doubtful _____

9. ABBREVIATIONS

Find the meaning of the following abbreviations.

mpg _____   km _____

i.e. _____   Ph.D. _____

10. NAMES OF PEOPLE

The names of famous people will be found either in the main part of your dictionary or in a separate biographical names section at the back.

Identify the following.

Thoreau _____

Chaucer _____

Longfellow _____

11. NAMES OF PLACES

The names of places will be found either in the main part of your dictionary or in a separate geographical names section at the back.

Identify the following.

Gibraltar _____

Karnak _____

Kilauea _____

12. FOREIGN WORDS AND PHRASES

Give the language and the meaning of the italicized expressions.

1. As I left, he waved and shouted, *"Auf Wiedersehen,"* _____

_____

2. The foreign government announced that the U.S. diplomat was

   persona non grata. _____

3. I had a feeling of *déjà vu* when I read his paper. _____

_____

13. MISCELLANEOUS INFORMATION

Find these miscellaneous bits of information in your dictionary.

1. When was Pompeii destroyed? _____

2. How long is the Suez Canal? _____

3. What is the capital of Manitoba? _____

4. A kilometer is equal to what portion of a mile? _____

5. When did Nebuchadnezzar die? _____

6. What is the plural of *cupful?* _____

7. What is the source of penicillin? _____

8. Near what country is the Great Barrier Reef? _____

9. What is the meaning of the British term *petrol?* _____

Sentence Structure

2

2 Sentence Structure

Among the most common errors in writing are fragments and run-together sentences. Here are some fragments:

> Having decided to drive to the mountains that afternoon
> Although we had never been on that road before
> The problem that bothered her the most

They don't make complete statements. They leave the reader wanting something more.

Here are some run-together sentences:

> I phoned Wendy she wasn't in.
> No one was in everybody had gone to the game.
> I finished my paper then I had a snack.

Unlike fragments, they make complete statements, but the trouble is they make *two* complete statements, which shouldn't be run together into one sentence without correct punctuation. The reader has to go back to see where there should have been a break.

Both fragments and run-together sentences confuse the reader. Not until you get rid of them will your writing be clear and easy to read. Unfortunately there is no quick, easy way to learn to avoid them. You have to learn a little about sentence structure to be sure that every sentence contains a subject and a verb.

FINDING SUBJECTS AND VERBS

When you write a sentence, you write about *something* or *someone.* That's the subject. Then you write what the subject *does* or *is.* That's the verb.

Birds fly.

The word *Birds* is the something you are writing about. It's the subject, and we'll underline it once. *Fly* tells what the subject does. It shows the action in the sentence. It's the verb, and we'll underline it twice. Because the verb often shows action, it's easier to spot than the subject. Therefore always look for it first. For example, in the sentence

Pat drives a delivery truck on Saturdays.

which word shows the action? Drives. It's the verb: Underline it twice. Now ask yourself who or what drives. Pat. It's the subject. Underline it once.

Study the following sentences until you understand how to pick out subjects and verbs.

Last night the rain flooded our basement. (Which word shows the action? Flooded. It's the verb. Underline it twice. Who or what flooded? Rain. It's the subject. Underline it once.)

Yesterday my brother ran in the five-mile relay. (Which word shows the action? Ran. Who or what ran? Brother.)

This year my sister plays the cello in the high school orchestra. (Which word shows the action? Plays. Who or what plays? Sister.)

Often the verb doesn't show action but merely tells what the subject *is* or *was.* Learn to spot such verbs—*is, are, was, were, seems, appears, becomes, looks . . .*

Dick is a trapeze artist. (First spot the verb is. Then ask who or what is. Dick is.)

Sheryl seems content in her new job. (First spot the verb seems. Then ask who or what seems. Sheryl seems.)

Sometimes the subject comes after the verb.

In the stands were five thousand spectators. (Who or what were in the stands? Spectators were.)

Where is the fire? (Who or what is? Fire is.)

There was a large crowd at the game. (Who or what was there? Crowd was there.)

There were not nearly enough seats for everybody. (Who or what were there? Seats were there.)

Here are my reasons. (Who or what are here? Reasons are here.)

Note that *there* and *here* (as in the last three sentences) are never subjects. They simply point out something.

In commands the subject often is not expressed. It is *you* (understood).

Come here. (You come here.)

Give me a hand. (You give me a hand.)

Eat your dinner. (You eat your dinner.)

As you pick out subjects in the following exercises, you may wonder whether you should say the subject is, for example, *trees* or *redwood trees*. It makes no difference so long as you get the main subject, *trees*, right. In the answers at the back of the book, usually—but not always—the single word is used. Don't waste your time worrying whether to include an extra word with the subject. Just make sure you get the main subject right.

EXERCISES

Underline the subject once and the verb twice. Find the verb first, and then ask **Who** or **What.** When you've finished ten sentences, compare your answers carefully with those at the back of the book.

□EXERCISE 1

1. Redwood trees are enormous.
2. They grow as high as 360 feet.
3. They are the largest living things in the world today.
4. Redwoods grow in a limited area along the coast of California.
5. They resist decay.
6. Their bark resists fire.
7. Therefore redwood trees live a long time.
8. Some are as much as four thousand years old.
9. Many were here at the time of Columbus.
10. Their wood varies in color from light cherry to dark mahogany.

□EXERCISE 2

1. From the top of a small hill we saw the prairie fire.
2. The fire swept across the dry land.
3. First there was only smoke.
4. Then there were a few flames.
5. Higher and higher rose the flames.
6. Fortunately a motorist saw the fire.
7. Minutes later he alerted the fire department in a nearby town.
8. Fire fighters spread out across the prairie.
9. They soon had the fire under control.
10. Only a small cabin on the edge of the prairie burned.

□EXERCISE 3

1. There was not a cloud in the sky.
2. A lizard darted from cactus to cactus.
3. Locusts swarmed over the prairie like a thundercloud.
4. Louder and louder grew the sound of the insects.
5. Here and there we saw prairie flowers.
6. The wind shifted the prairie soil constantly.
7. In the distance rose the majestic mountains.
8. The sun sank rapidly below the horizon.
9. Then the prairie suddenly became cold.
10. We were glad for the warmth of our car.

□EXERCISE 4

1. The koala is always popular in any zoo.
2. It is a native of Australia.
3. The koala looks a bit like a teddy bear.
4. No other plant-eating animal has such a restricted diet.
5. Its food consists almost exclusively of leaves of the eucalyptus tree.
6. But now fewer eucalyptus forests exist.
7. And the koala population dwindles.
8. A newborn koala is about an inch long.
9. It crawls into its mother's pouch for further development.
10. At six months the fully developed koala rides on its mother's shoulders.

□EXERCISE 5

1. Every state in the Union now has a state bird.
2. The cardinal is the most popular.
3. Seven states chose it as their state bird.
4. Those states are Kentucky, Illinois, Indiana, Ohio, North Carolina, Virginia, and West Virginia.

5. The second most popular bird is the western meadowlark.
6. It belongs to Kansas, Wyoming, Nebraska, Montana, North Dakota, and Oregon.
7. The Hawaiian nene is on the endangered species list.
8. The smallest state bird is the black-capped chickadee of Maine and Massachusetts.
9. The cactus wren was a natural choice for Arizona.
10. Perhaps the most beautiful state bird is the ring-necked pheasant of South Dakota.

□EXERCISE 6

1. Oceans cover 71 percent of the surface of the earth.
2. The five oceans are the Pacific, Atlantic, Indian, Arctic, and Antarctic.
3. The waters of all five oceans join.
4. Therefore they really make one great ocean.
5. The oceans are actually a part of each of us.
6. Our body fluids are chemically similar to seawater.
7. This is probably an inheritance from our sea-living ancestors.
8. The oceans give life to the earth.
9. They send moisture into the clouds.
10. The clouds then supply us with life-sustaining water.

□EXERCISE 7

1. The sea gives us food, medicines, minerals, and fertilizers.
2. About one-fifth of the world's oil and gas comes from under the sea.
3. Many people like to live by the sea.
4. Of the U.S. population, 30 percent live within fifty miles of the sea.
5. The sea also provides a playground for people.
6. People like to play either on or in the sea.
7. Playing on the sea includes swimming, boating, surfing, fishing, and cruising.
8. Playing in the sea includes snorkeling and scuba diving.
9. Some divers explore the sea-plant forests to take pictures.
10. Others hunt for sunken treasure.

□EXERCISE 8

1. Last summer I took a trip to Washington, D.C.
2. There I visited the National Gallery of Art.
3. It contains some of our country's greatest art treasures.
4. I learned some things about the Impressionist and Postimpressionist painters.
5. Seurat used tiny daubs of pure color in his paintings.
6. Picasso burned his sketches for warmth during his early years.

7. Van Gogh often applied paint to the canvas with a pallet knife.
8. The paintings by Van Gogh interested me especially.
9. Before leaving, I bought a Van Gogh print.
10. Try to visit the National Gallery someday.

□EXERCISE 9

1. I never knew anything about left-handed people.
2. But I recently read an article about them.
3. It was in the December 1994 *Smithsonian* magazine.
4. Ten to fifteen percent of humans are left-handed.
5. Three former presidents were left-handed: George Bush, Harry Truman, and Gerald Ford.
6. Today on television you probably saw President Bill Clinton jot down some notes with a pencil in his left hand.
7. Of the great left-handed painters Leonardo, Raphael, Holbein, and Picasso are the most famous.
8. Harpo Marx and Charlie Chaplin were left-handed actors.
9. Chaplin played a custom-made, left-handed violin.
10. Now I have a great new admiration for left-handed people.

WRITING ASSIGNMENT

As you get back your writing assignments, are you keeping a list of your misspelled words on the inside back cover of this book?

Proofreading Exercise

In these paragraphs are errors from all the material you've studied. Can you find ten errors? Challenge your instructor to find ten on the first try. No answers are provided at the back of the book for this exercise.

EVERGREENS

The oldest, the tallest, and the most massive living things are the evergreens. The oldest our the bristlecone pines, which grow in Great Basin National Park in Nevada. These evergreens were all ready seedlings when the Egyptians were building the Great Pyramid more then four thousand years ago. Since than, civilizations have risen and fallen, but these same bristlecone pines are still living. The oldest of all of them is one nicknamed Methuselah, which scientists have determined from it's rings to be 4,600 years old.

The tallest living thing is also a evergreen. Its a coast redwood standing 367.8 feet high in Humboldt County, California. Thats as tall as a skyscraper.

The most massive living thing on earth is another redwood—the General Sherman in Sequoia National Park, with a trunk girth of 79.8 feet, a height of 267 feet, and a estimated weight including the root system of 6,720 tons. A seed from that tree, however, weighs only one-six-thousandth of a ounce.

Viewing such trees is an unforgettable experience.

SUBJECTS ARE NOT IN PREPOSITIONAL PHRASES

A prepositional phrase is simply a preposition and the name of someone or something. (See the examples in the columns below.) We don't use many grammatical terms in this book, and the only reason we're mentioning prepositional phrases is to get them out of the way. Without them you can identify the subject and verb of a sentence more easily. For example, you might have difficulty finding the subject and verb in a long sentence like this:

> During the summer one of my friends drove to her parents' home near Missoula in western Montana.

But if you cross out all the prepositional phrases like this:

> ~~During the summer~~ one ~~of my friends~~ drove ~~to her parents' home near Missoula in western Montana.~~

then you have only two words left—the subject and the verb. Even in short sentences like the following, you might pick the wrong word as the subject if you didn't cross out the prepositional phrases first.

> One ~~of my friends~~ lives ~~in Oxnard, California.~~
>
> Most ~~of the team~~ went ~~on the trip.~~

The subject is never in a prepositional phrase. Read this list to learn to recognize prepositional phrases.

about the desk	**by** the desk	**outside** the desk
above the desk	**down** the street	**over** the desk
across the desk	**during** vacation	**past** the desk
after vacation	**except** the desk	**since** vacation
against the desk	**for** the desk	**through** the desk
along the street	**from** the desk	**throughout** the vacation
among the desks	**in** the desk	**to** the desk
around the desk	**inside** the desk	**toward** the desk
at the desk	**into** the desk	**under** the desk
before vacation	**like** the desk	**underneath** the desk
behind the desk	**near** the desk	**until** vacation
below the desk	**of** the desk	**up** the street
beneath the desk	**off** the desk	**upon** the desk
beside the desk	**on** the desk	**with** the desk
between the desks	**onto** the desk	**within** the desk
beyond the desk	**out** the window	

NOTE: Don't mistake *to* plus a verb for a prepositional phrase. For example, *to run* is not a prepositional phrase because *run* is not the name of something. It's a verb.

EXERCISES

Cross out the prepositional phrases. Then underline the subject once and the verb twice. Correct each group of ten sentences before continuing.

☐EXERCISE 1

1. One of the latest fads on college campuses is juggling.
2. The art of juggling is inexpensive and easy to learn.
3. At MIT jugglers pass clubs in complicated patterns.
4. At the Williams College commencement in 1984, a graduate accepted his diploma.
5. Then he lit three torches for a spectacular juggling display for the audience.
6. The members of the International Jugglers Association number almost three thousand.
7. Eighty percent of the jugglers are amateurs.
8. In Tonga women jugglers keep seven limes or green tui tui nuts airborne.
9. A Guinness record for juggled objects is eleven rings in motion by a juggler in Russia in 1973.
10. Anthony Gott holds a Guinness record for juggling seven flaming torches in 1989.

☐EXERCISE 2

1. Hibernation differs from sleep.
2. In sleep animals merely relax.
3. In hibernation, however, their life almost stops.
4. The breathing of the animals becomes very slow.
5. The beating of their hearts becomes irregular.
6. During hibernation, a woodchuck's body is only a little warmer than the air in its burrow.
7. Some kinds of insects freeze almost solid.
8. In preparing for hibernation, mammals generally eat large amounts of food.
9. They store the food in thick layers of fat.
10. Groundhogs, for example, become very plump before hibernation.

□EXERCISE 3

1. The national bird of the United States is the bald eagle.
2. With its white head and white tail feathers, it is easy to identify.
3. But bald eagles are now an endangered species.
4. Cedar Glen along the Mississippi River in Illinois is a haven for them.
5. An area of 580 acres around Cedar Glen is now one of the largest eagle sanctuaries in the country.
6. After their breeding season in the northern states and Canada, approximately 300 eagles gather at Cedar Glen for the winter.
7. For five or six months each winter they stay in this protected place.
8. On frigid winter nights the eagles perch beside each other on the branches of large sycamore trees.
9. More bald eagles spend the winter at Cedar Glen than at any other place in the Midwest.
10. Havens like this ensure a future for our national bird.

□EXERCISE 4

1. Of all the states in the Union, Alaska is the largest.
2. One of its most impressive features is the nation's tallest mountain.
3. Alaskans call the mountain Denali, a Native American word for "great one."
4. Of all our national forests, Alaska has the largest—the Tongass National Forest with seventeen million acres.
5. In that forest are four-hundred-year-old Sitka spruces.
6. Now the pristine beauty of Alaska is threatened by lumbering interests and oil companies.
7. Loggers have already cut approximately 300,000 acres of the Tongass Forest.
8. The lumber companies cut approximately 10,000 acres of old-growth evergreens each year.
9. Furthermore, oil interests want to build a new natural gas pipeline for bringing gas from Prudhoe Bay to market.
10. It is a question of providing economic growth versus protecting an invaluable wildlife reserve.

Source: *National Wildlife,* June–July, 1990

□EXERCISE 5

1. On a backpacking trip to Alaska, we visited Admiralty Island National Monument.
2. With no changes since the end of the last Ice Age, the island stands in its original grandeur.

3. In the center of the island, rugged snowcapped peaks rise five thousand feet above the magnificent forests.
4. The natives call the island "The Fortress of the Bears."
5. It is home to approximately a thousand Alaskan brown bears or grizzlies.
6. Along the shores are havens for young salmon and king crab.
7. Admiralty Island is one of the few totally natural areas left in this country.
8. But now a logging firm wants to cut 23,000 acres of virgin timber on the island and to build a logging transfer terminal on the shore.
9. Congress passed the Alaska Lands Act in 1980 to protect such areas.
10. It often takes years of legal battles, however, to halt the loggers.

□EXERCISE 6

1. Last year there was a labor dispute on our campus here in Vancouver.
2. The campus maintenance workers, with the approval of their labor union, threatened to strike and to shut down the whole campus.
3. Many of the students supported the workers.
4. They forgot about losing their entire semester's credits.
5. Also there were only a few maintenance workers in contrast to two thousand students.
6. I decided to write a letter to the campus newspaper and also one to the city paper.
7. Then I circulated a petition on campus about students' rights.
8. I explained the students' concern about losing a semester's credit.
9. Luckily the two sides reached a settlement quickly with no classes disrupted.
10. Participating in campus politics is both enjoyable and worthwhile.

MORE ABOUT VERBS AND SUBJECTS

Sometimes the verb is more than one word. Here are a few of the many forms of the verb *drive:*

I drive	I will be driving	I may drive
I am driving	I will have been driving	I could drive
I have driven	I will have driven	I might drive
I have been driving	I am driven	I should drive
I drove	I was driven	I would drive
I was driving	I have been driven	I must drive
I had driven	I had been driven	I could have driven
I had been driving	I will be driven	I might have driven
I will drive	I can drive	I should have driven

Note that words like the following are never part of the verb even though they may be in the middle of the verb:

already	ever	not	really
also	finally	now	sometimes
always	just	often	usually
even	never	only	

Amy had never driven to the city before. She had always taken the bus.

Two verb forms—*driving* and *to drive*—look like verbs, but neither can ever be the verb of a sentence. No *ing* word by itself can ever be the verb of a sentence; it must have a helping verb in front of it.

Pablo driving home (not a sentence because there is no proper verb)
Pablo was driving home. (a sentence)

And no verb with *to* in front of it can ever be the verb of a sentence.

To drive down the river road (not a sentence because there is no proper verb and no subject)

I like to drive down the river road. (a sentence with *like* as the verb)

She wants to go to college to become an engineer. (a sentence with *wants* as the verb)

These two forms, *driving* and *to drive,* may be used as subjects, or they may have other uses in the sentence.

Driving is fun.   To drive is fun.   We practiced on the driving range.

But neither of them can ever be the verb of a sentence.

Not only may a verb be composed of more than one word, but also there may be more than one verb in a sentence:

Kevin painted the house and planted trees in the yard.

The children jumped up and down, shouted, and clapped their hands.

Also there may be more than one subject.

Kevin and Natalie painted the house and planted trees in the yard.

José, Patti, Jennifer, and Sean came to the party.

EXERCISES

Underline the subject once and the verb twice. Be sure to include all parts of the verb. Also watch for more than one subject and more than one verb. It's a good idea to cross out the prepositional phrases first.

□EXERCISE 1

1. The largest library in the world is the Library of Congress in Washington, D.C.
2. It contains 535 miles of shelves and holds over 25 million items.
3. Each day over 31,000 new books, periodicals, and recordings pour into the library.
4. Three-quarters of the 800 million books are written in one of 470 foreign languages.
5. By 1865 the two library buildings were overflowing.
6. Then in 1880 the James Madison Memorial Library was completed.
7. It is larger than the first two buildings combined and also is the largest single library building in the world.
8. The library has four million maps inside two acres of storage cabinets.
9. There are maps of the moon, a sailor's chart of the Mediterranean drawn on sheepskin between 1320 and 1350, and a 17th-century map showing California as a giant island.
10. Each year library employees send recordings, tapes, and Braille literature to over 700,000 of the nation's blind and physically handicapped.

□EXERCISE 2

1. The most famous book in the Library of Congress is the Gutenberg Bible from 1455.
2. That volume is one of three surviving copies in the world and was the first book ever printed with movable type.
3. The papers of 23 American presidents are stored in the library.
4. The library contains Jefferson's first draft of the Declaration of Independence with handwritten notes by Benjamin Franklin and John Adams.
5. Four million pieces of music from classical to rock are found there.
6. A collection of rare Stradivarius violins is also included.
7. The Orville and Wilbur Wright collection features the historic photo of the first powered flight near Kitty Hawk, NC in 1903.
8. The Library of Congress has now become a library for all Americans.
9. Libraries from all over the country can borrow books from it.
10. Visit the Library of Congress some day and take one of the free tours.

□EXERCISE 3

1. I have been reading about the whooping crane.
2. The whooping crane is a tall white bird with a red crown.
3. Once there were hundreds of whooping cranes.
4. Then their numbers declined because of hunting and because of the destruction of the prairie wetlands in the Midwest.
5. Also the roosting sites along their migratory route were disturbed by the construction of new roads.
6. Eventually only 18 whooping cranes were left.
7. Then the Canadian National Railway planned to build a branch line in the nesting area of the whooping cranes.
8. Environmentalists, however, got the Railroad to change its route.
9. Now some of the key stopover sites of the cranes are being protected.
10. And once again hundreds of whooping cranes can be seen in the wild.

□EXERCISE 4

1. One of the strangest animals is the tassel-eared squirrel in the pine forests of the Southern Rockies.
2. The tassel-eared squirrel gets its name from the pointed tufts of hair which sprout from its eartips prior to the breeding season.
3. During the summer this squirrel feeds on pine pollen, fungi, seeds, and buds just as many squirrels do.
4. But with the coming of autumn and throughout the winter the tassel-eared squirrel feeds only on the inner bark of the ponderosa pine.
5. The bark is gummy, stringy, and not very nutritious.

6. Few animals are as dependent on a particular plant or tree as the tassel-eared squirrel.
7. It builds a bushel-basket-sized nest in the top of a ponderosa pine for the winter.
8. Then it lines the nest with pine needles and grasses from the forest floor.
9. In the spring mating occurs, and soon a litter of three to five babies is born.
10. The young remain in the nest for six or seven weeks before venturing forth.

□EXERCISE 5

1. I have just learned about animals playing games.
2. Of course I have always known about people's games.
3. But an article in the *National Geographic Explorer* tells about animals' games.
4. The urge to play is built into both human and animal genes.
5. By playing games animals and people learn to be adults.
6. Monkeys play leap frog and tug of war.
7. Other animals play ball and wrestle.
8. They learn to give clear signals to their companions.
9. Play is often related to survival.
10. It teaches animals how to get along with the rest of the pack.

JOURNAL WRITING

Write about something that interests you, using some of the words from your Spelling List on the inside back cover.

CORRECTING RUN-TOGETHER SENTENCES

Any group of words having a subject and verb is a clause. The clause may be independent (able to stand alone) or dependent (unable to stand alone). Every sentence you have worked with so far has been an independent clause because it has been able to stand alone. It has made a complete statement.

If two independent clauses are written together with no punctuation or with a comma between them, they are called a run-together sentence. (Some textbooks call them a run-on sentence, a comma splice, or a comma fault.) Here are some examples.

He cooked the dinner she washed the dishes.
He cooked the dinner, she washed the dishes.
I like science fiction therefore I enjoyed the movie.
I like science fiction, therefore I enjoyed the movie.

Run-together sentences can be corrected in one of three ways:

1. Make the two independent clauses into two sentences.

He cooked the dinner. She washed the dishes.
I like science fiction. Therefore I enjoyed the movie.

2. Connect the two independent clauses with a semicolon.

He cooked the dinner; she washed the dishes.
I like science fiction; therefore I enjoyed the movie.
I turned my paper in; then I began to review.
I worked hard; thus I passed the test.

When a connecting word such as

also	however	otherwise
consequently	likewise	then
finally	moreover	therefore
furthermore	nevertheless	thus

is used between two independent clauses, it always has a semicolon before it, and it may have a comma after it, especially if there seems to be a pause between the word and the rest of the sentence.

The book was interesting; however, I didn't finish it.
I'll enjoy the job; furthermore, I need the money.

I want to go; also, I think it's my duty.
The attendance was small; nevertheless, a lot was accomplished.

The semicolon before the connecting word is required. The comma after it is a matter of choice.

3. Connect the two independent clauses with a comma and one of the following words: *and, but, for, or, nor, yet, so.*

The library book sale is today, *and* I'm going to help.
I don't want to, *but* I think I should.
I gave my promise, *for* they need help.
I must hurry, *or* I won't be on time.
I must study, *so* I can get good grades.

But be sure there are two independent clauses. The first sentence below has two independent clauses. The second sentence is merely one independent clause with two verbs, and therefore no comma should be used.

He jogged two kilometers, and then he went for a swim.

He jogged two kilometers and then went for a swim.

THE THREE WAYS TO PUNCTUATE INDEPENDENT CLAUSES

She went to the library. She needed to study.
She went to the library; she needed to study.
She went to the library, for she needed to study.

Learn these three ways, and you'll avoid run-together sentences. (On page 80, you'll learn a fourth way.)

You may wonder when to use a period and capital letter and when to use a semicolon between two independent clauses. In general, use a period and capital letter. Only if the clauses are very closely related in meaning should you use a semicolon.

EXERCISES

In each independent clause underline the subject once and the verb twice. Then be ready to give a reason for the punctuation.

☐EXERCISE 1

1. I am writing a term paper on Arthur Erickson; he is a famous Canadian architect.
2. He has designed universities and public buildings, and at Japan's Expo '70 he won the top architectural award over entries from seventy-eight countries.
3. He has designed a three-block complex in downtown Vancouver. His achievement has restored vitality to the downtown area.
4. The complex consists of buildings and plazas, and it has the most extensive urban planting of trees, shrubs, and vines of any North American city.
5. A luxurious office building for the local government and a seven-story courthouse are included in the complex.
6. The courthouse is more open and less forbidding than most courthouses, and its glass roof is one of the biggest in the world.
7. Robson Square is the greatest attraction, for it is a place for outdoor lunches, shows, and theater groups.
8. Robson Square also has an outdoor ice- or roller-skating rink as well as indoor theaters, restaurants, and an exhibition hall.
9. An energy tank for the complex is heated or cooled during cheaper off-peak hours, and the buildings are then heated or cooled from the tank.
10. Most of Erickson's work has been in Canada, but his latest project is the Canadian Embassy in Washington, D.C.

Most—but not all—of the following sentences are run-together. If the sentence has two independent clauses, separate them with the correct punctuation—comma, semicolon, or period with a capital letter. In general, use the period with a capital letter rather than the semicolon. But either way is correct. Thus your answers may differ from those at the back of the book.

☐EXERCISE 2

1. I never knew much about the Statue of Liberty then at the time of its one hundredth birthday in 1986 I read an article about it.
2. It was a gift from the French people they contributed the funds for its construction in Paris.

3. It commemorates the friendship of the people of France and the people of the United States.
4. It was made of hundreds of copper sheets each was hammered into shape by hand.
5. Finally it was finished then it was disassembled and shipped to New York.
6. It now faces down the New York Harbor thus voyagers on arrival see it as a symbol of freedom and opportunity.
7. The statue is 305 feet high she holds a torch in her right hand.
8. In her left hand she holds a tablet it contains the inscription "July 4, 1776."
9. On her head a crown with seven spokes represents the seven seas and the seven continents and at her feet lie the broken shackles of slavery.
10. An elevator and a spiral staircase lead to an observation platform in the crown I hope to see the view from there someday.

☐EXERCISE 3

1. Grizzly bears are causing problems and conservationists are worried.
2. In the 1800s there were fifty thousand grizzlies in the West now there are fewer than one thousand.
3. Approximately two hundred of those grizzlies live in and near Yellowstone National Park and formerly they caused no trouble.
4. But in 1967 the Park Service decided to keep the park natural and the garbage dumps were closed.
5. Hotelkeepers were no longer allowed to put out food to attract the bears and the bears had to fend for themselves.
6. The Park Service meant well but the new rules had unexpected consequences.
7. The bears began to look for food in campgrounds and they killed sheep on nearby farms.
8. They began prowling in mining camps and near vacation homes and maulings and even deaths occurred.
9. The Park Service refuses to reopen the old dumps but they are going to leave food out for the bears in certain places.
10. The grizzlies won't change their habits therefore humans must change theirs.

☐EXERCISE 4

1. One of the most popular museums in Washington, D.C., is the National Air and Space Museum it portrays the age of the airplane from the flight of the Wright brothers to today's space exploration.

2. Here may be seen the Wright brothers' original 1903 Flyer and Lindbergh's *Spirit of St. Louis* here too visitors may touch a rock from the moon.

3. In all there are more than two hundred original airplanes and spacecraft they are housed in a three-block-long marble building.

4. Each of the largest galleries is more than six stories high and three times larger than a basketball court.

5. Three of these galleries house historic aircraft such as the linked *Apollo-Soyuz Spacecraft* and the *Skylab Orbital Workshop* here also are historic commercial airliners.

6. The exhibits are either suspended from the glass-roofed ceiling or else they seem to rise from below the floor level.

7. Smaller galleries show examples of vertical flight: balloons, combat flying in World War I, air traffic control, and man-made satellites.

8. The motion picture *To Fly* is sensational it begins with a balloon ascension in 1831 and ends with a voyage to outer space.

9. In the film the viewer feels the thrill of flying upside down or of sailing along in a tiny hang glider.

10. An average of nine million people visit the museum each year it is part of the great Smithsonian Institution.

□EXERCISE 5

1. Dinosaurs! I had never thought much about them I knew only that they were big animals from the distant past.

2. But now I've read an article about them in the *National Geographic* and I've learned a lot.

3. The word *dinosaur* comes from *deinos* meaning "terrible" and *sauros* meaning "lizard" thus dinosaurs were "terrible lizards."

4. They were enormous creatures that lived some 230 million years ago and paleontologists are now unearthing many of their skeletons.

5. I had always assumed that dinosaur bones had been found in only a few countries but now I've learned that paleontologists are unearthing skeletons all over the world—even in Antarctica.

6. Dinosaurs flourished for 165 million years and then they disappeared.

7. But no one knows why they disappeared.

8. Dinosaurs lived even in Alaska 66 million years ago but how did they survive the winters?

9. Did they remain there when the winter's darkness and cold descended upon them or did they migrate south?

10. No one knows excavating their skeletons gives no clues.

□EXERCISE 6

1. Excavating dinosaur skeletons is a tedious process a paleontologist in New Mexico is working to free a dinosaur from hard sandstone.
2. He is using a mirror and dental pick to free the smaller parts his job will take years.
3. One of the world's richest concentrations of dinosaur footprints is found on the South Korean coast they are embedded in petrified mud.
4. And in Dinosaur Provincial Park near Calgary, Alberta, Canada, more than fifteen different dinosaur species have been found.
5. This part of Alberta may have been a stopover for herds of dinosaurs migrating to Alaska or it may have been a wintering site.
6. Brown scraps of dinosaur bones litter the ground there and protrude from the eroded hillsides.
7. Teeth too are found there a dinosaur was always losing teeth and then growing more.
8. The Dakotas and Montana contain one of the few rock formations on earth that record in detail the great beasts' final two million years.
9. The largest dinosaur ever displayed is the Brachiosaurus in a museum in Berlin it may have weighed eighty tons when alive.
10. More and more excavation continues we want to know more about the early inhabitants of our Earth.

Source: *National Geographic*, January 1993

Punctuate the following paragraphs so there will be no run-together sentences.

□EXERCISE 7

1. Last spring we were driving through Arizona and decided to see the Petrified Forest therefore we took the twenty-seven-mile drive through that strange landscape trees have turned to stone and thousands of great stone logs lie on the ground we learned a great deal about petrified wood and were glad for the experience the National Park Service is preserving the area for future generations.
2. Bicycling is *the* mode of travel today. More than ten million cycles were sold in 1989 and eighty-four million cyclists are now pedaling on a regular basis as many women as men cycle and for the first time in history adult riders outnumber kids becoming popular are the long non-competitive bicycle rides like the 495-mile "Annual Great Bicycle Ride Across Iowa" and the "Hotter 'N Hell Hundred" starting in Waco, Texas probably the longest ride is the "Pedal for Power" from Maine to Florida. Yes, bicycling is in.

3. A car running on a tankful of sunshine? Yes, it has happened students from thirty-two colleges designed their cars to capture the sun's rays then the cars' photovoltaic cells converted the rays into electricity to run the motors. The students took part in the 1,641-mile "GM Sunrayce USA" from Florida to Michigan it was the largest rally ever held for sun-powered cars. Of course the internal combustion engine won't soon be replaced by a tankful of sunshine but the Sunrayce did point the way to more aerodynamic car designs for saving fuel.

Source: *Newsweek,* July 23, 1990

JOURNAL WRITING

Write three sentences illustrating the three ways of punctuating two independent clauses.

CORRECTING FRAGMENTS

There are two kinds of clauses: independent (which we have just finished studying) and dependent. A dependent clause has a subject and a verb just like an independent clause, but it can't stand alone because it begins with a dependent word (or words) such as

after	since	whereas
although	so that	wherever
as	than	whether
as if	that	which
because	though	whichever
before	unless	while
even if	until	who
even though	what	whom
ever since	whatever	whose
how	when	why
if	whenever	
in order that	where	

Whenever a clause begins with one of the above dependent words (unless it's a question, which would be followed by a question mark), it is dependent.

Note that *after, before, since,* and *until* function differently as prepositions.

If we take an independent clause such as

We finished the game.

and put one of the dependent words in front of it, it becomes a dependent clause and cannot stand alone:

After we finished the game
Although we finished the game
As we finished the game
Before we finished the game
Since we finished the game
That we finished the game
When we finished the game
While we finished the game

As you read the clause, you can hear that it doesn't make a complete statement. It leaves the reader expecting something more. Therefore it can no longer stand alone. A dependent clause is a fragment and must not be punctuated as a sentence. To correct such a fragment, add an independent clause:

After we finished the game, we went to the clubhouse.
We went to the clubhouse after we finished the game.
We were happy that we finished the game early.
While we finished the game, the others waited.

In other words **EVERY SENTENCE MUST HAVE AT LEAST ONE INDEPENDENT CLAUSE.**

Note in the examples that **when a dependent clause comes at the beginning of a sentence, it is followed by a comma.** Often the comma prevents misreading, as in the following sentence:

When he entered, the refrigerator door was open.

Without a comma after *entered,* the reader would read *When he entered the refrigerator* before realizing that that was not what the author meant. The comma prevents misreading. Sometimes if the dependent clause is short and there is no danger of misreading, the comma is omitted, but it's safer simply to follow the rule that a dependent clause at the beginning of a sentence is followed by a comma.

You'll learn more about the punctuation of dependent clauses on page 161, but right now just remember the above rule.

Note that sometimes the dependent word is the subject of the dependent clause:

I took the highway that was finished just last month.

I don't know what is wrong.

Sometimes the dependent clause is in the middle of the independent clause:

The highway that was finished last month goes to Cincinnati.

The problem that is facing us is easy to solve.

And sometimes the dependent clause is the subject of the entire sentence:

What I was doing was not important.

Where you're going on vacation interests me.

Whatever you decide is fine.

Also note that sometimes the *that* of a dependent clause is omitted.

This is the house that Jack built.

This is the house Jack built.

I thought that you were coming with me.

I thought you were coming with me.

The word *that* doesn't always introduce a dependent clause. It may be a pronoun and serve as the subject of the sentence.

That is my book.
That is familiar.

That can also be a describing word.

I like that book.
That photo is beautiful.

EXERCISES

Underline the subject once and the verb twice in both the independent and the dependent clauses. Then put a broken line under the dependent clause.

☐EXERCISE 1

1. Yesterday I went to a museum where I learned a lot.

2. I learned that corals are animals.

3. I had always thought that they were plants.

4. I learned that there are 800,000 species of insects on earth.

5. That is more than if we counted all other animals and plants together.

6. Mammals are the only animals that suckle their young.

7. And bats are the only mammals that fly.

8. I learned more than I had expected to on that visit.

9. If you want to broaden your knowledge, you should go to a museum.

10. What you can learn is amazing.

Underline each dependent clause with a broken line.

□EXERCISE 2

1. When a leaf falls from a tree, it has no further value.
2. That is what I thought.
3. Now I have learned that a leaf still has value.
4. When it falls into a stream, it is eaten by small insects that are called shredders.
5. The shredders that eat the soft part of the leaf leave the hard veins.
6. Then fish eat the shredders that have eaten the leaf.
7. Next a fisherman catches the fish that has eaten the shredders.
8. He then sells the fish to a sportsman who has not been lucky in his fishing.
9. The sportsman proudly carries home the fish, which is then eaten by his family.
10. Thus a fallen leaf does have value because it has become food for insects, fish, and also people.

Source: *National Wildlife,* Oct.–Nov. 1987

□EXERCISE 3

1. When I go out on a dark evening, I look up at the sky.
2. If I take the time, I can usually find quite a few constellations.
3. As the weeks go by, I'm adding a few more constellations to my list.
4. If I'm on campus in the evening, I look at the stars through the telescope.
5. I wish that I had taken my astronomy course sooner.
6. It has taught me many things that I had never imagined before.
7. Astronomers have located a quasar that may be the largest object in the universe.
8. Whereas the Earth's diameter is about 8,000 miles, the diameter of the newly discovered quasar is 468,000,000 miles.
9. If you stood on the moon and looked back toward Earth, you could see with the naked eye only one man-made structure.
10. The structure that you would see is the Great Wall of China.

If the clause is independent and therefore a sentence, put a period after it. If the clause is dependent and therefore a fragment, add an independent clause either before or after it to make it into a sentence. Remember that if the dependent clause comes first, it should have a comma after it.

□EXERCISE 4

1. As he ran to catch the ball

2. Then he finally caught it

3. She couldn't find the necessary reference material

4. Because no one had told me about the new ruling

5. When I finally decide to really work

6. Therefore I'm going to stay at home tonight

7. If I can just spend a couple of hours on my math

8. Moreover I should study my psychology

9. When I'm finished with both of them

10. I'll feel confident about those tests

On pages 69–70 you learned three ways of correcting run-together sentences. Now that you are aware of dependent clauses, you can use a fourth way. In the following run-together sentence

The snow was beginning to melt we canceled our ski trip.

you can make one of the two independent clauses into a dependent clause by putting a dependent word in front of it, as in the following examples:

Because the snow was beginning to melt, we canceled our ski trip.
We canceled our ski trip since the snow was beginning to melt.
When the snow began to melt, we canceled our ski trip.

This fourth way of correcting a run-together sentence is often the best because it puts the more important of the two ideas in the independent clause and thus makes it stand out.

Correct the following run-together sentences by making one of the clauses dependent. In some sentences you will want to put the dependent clause first; in others you may want to put it last or in the middle of the sentence. Since various words can be used to start a dependent clause, your answers may differ from those suggested at the back of the book.

☐EXERCISE 5

1. Last summer a friend and I took a trip across western Canada we had never been there before.

2. We drove from Winnipeg to Vancouver it was almost 2,500 kilometers.

3. We saw many interesting things we'll not soon forget them.

4. The most interesting of all was the Tyrrell Museum of Paleontology it's in the Province of Alberta near the little town of Drumheller.

5. I have now learned the meaning of *paleontology* it's the study of ancient life through the study of fossils.

6. The museum is named for Joseph B. Tyrrell he discovered the first dinosaur bones in the area.

7. Tyrrell was a geologist he was hunting coal deposits.

8. One day in 1884 he was looking for veins of coal he accidentally uncovered a dinosaur skull.

9. The museum was opened in 1985 and contains thirty-five complete dinosaur skeletons that is the largest number assembled under one roof anywhere in the world.

10. Now we can learn about dinosaurs they roamed the earth for 140 million years.

□EXERCISE 6

1. In the Tyrrell Museum we also learned about 3.5 million years of the Earth's history that history extends from the time of the first forms of life to the emergence of the dinosaurs to the world today.

2. The most striking thing about the dinosaurs in Alberta is their lifestyles they were surprisingly different from each other.

3. Some dinosaurs laid eggs some are thought to have borne live young.

4. Some migrated as far as two thousand miles a year others traveled from coastal feeding grounds to mountain heights to breed and hatch their young.

5. Some were cold-blooded some were warm-blooded.

6. An indoor garden in the museum houses 110 species of plants the plants are all related to those of dinosaur times.

7. Some of the plants merely resemble those of dinosaur times others have remained virtually unchanged since those days.

8. More than half a million people annually visit the museum it is one of the largest paleontological museums in the world.

9. We learned much about dinosaurs during our day there we left wondering about the still unsolved mystery of the sudden disappearance of the dinosaurs.

10. The next day we continued our motor trip we couldn't quit talking about the dinosaurs.

□EXERCISE 7

1. Some people have 20/20 vision that is said to be perfect eyesight.

2. Such vision is perfect for humans it may not be perfect for animals and birds.

3. Some birds have sharp vision it may be sharper than that of humans.

4. A hawk might be perched on top of the Empire State Building it could see a worm on the sidewalk below.

5. A hawk has a vision eight times greater than that of humans it is thus able to scan fields for prey.

6. A frog has a different kind of vision it sees things as a constant motion picture.

7. The cells in a frog's eyes have been called bug detectors they respond mainly to moving objects.

8. The frog sees the tiny movement of bugs the human eye could not detect such tiny movements.

9. But a frog might be sitting in a field of dead bugs it might fail to see them and perhaps starve.

10. Human eyesight is rather limited compared to that of other species only humans and some other primates can see color.

Source: *Science Digest*, July 1984

□EXERCISE 8

1. We think of apples as food for people animals like apples too.

2. Bears are led by their sense of smell they'll travel miles to find juicy apples.

3. Apple leaves are eaten by deer apple seeds are eaten by squirrels and birds.

4. Birds also eat young apple buds this has perturbed apple growers.

5. Now most apple growers accept the debudding actually it improves the size and quality of the remaining fruit.

6. Some trees hold their fruit all winter most let their fruit fall to the ground.

7. The apples on the ground rot they then enrich the soil.

8. Worms flourish in the enriched soil birds then gather to hunt the worms.

9. A nineteenth-century missionary from Massachusetts traveled across the country he planted and gave away apple seeds and seedlings.

10. The news of John Chapman's work spread he became known as Johnny Appleseed.

□EXERCISE 9

1. Thoreau said in 1854, "In wildness is the preservation of the world," the idea was not given much thought until the 1950s.

2. Then in the 1950s a plan was proposed to set aside vast tracts of public lands wildlife would be left in its natural condition.

3. The proposed Wilderness Act set off a bitter seven-year struggle in Congress the act had to be rewritten sixty-six times.

4. Finally the Wilderness Act of 1964 was passed about 9.1 million acres of national forest and park land became protected.

5. Public support grew almost 91 million acres are protected today.

6. Opponents of the act said it would deprive the country of mineral and timber resources there has been no such loss.

7. The unspoiled wilderness has tremendous economic value for recreation and tourism it also promotes the economy of surrounding areas.

8. The Wilderness Act of 1964 began the environmental movement the word *ecology* has now become a powerful idea.

9. There are still many areas to be preserved for example more than 12 million acres surrounding Yellowstone Park include critical habitat for grizzlies, bighorn sheep, elk, and wolves.

10. More than 90 million acres are now protected another 90 million qualify for protection.

Source: *National Wildlife*, Oct.–Nov. 1989

JOURNAL WRITING

Now that you're aware of independent and dependent clauses, you can vary your sentences. Write three sentences, each containing two independent clauses connected by one of the following words. Be sure to use the correct punctuation—comma or semicolon.

and	for	or
but	however	then
consequently	nevertheless	

Now rewrite the three sentences using one independent and one dependent clause in each. Use some of the following dependent words. If you put the dependent clause first, put a comma after it.

after	if	until
although	since	while
because	unless	

Proofreading Exercise

See if you can correct all five errors in this student paragraph. No answers are provided at the back of the book.

MY MOUNTAIN BIKE

Last year I bought a bicycle to get to school. Its a mountain bike with fat tires and fifteen gears and a really solid frame. It goes over curbs and bumps with no problem. This spring I decided to take it on some trails in the woods, and Ive been amazed at were I can go and what I can do. I can jump small logs and rocks on the trail. I can really move on the straight stretches, and in the lowest gear I can climb steep hills. Im having so much fun that people have been watching me, and now a lot of other mountain bikes our beginning to appear on the trails.

MORE ABOUT FRAGMENTS

We've seen that a dependent clause alone is a fragment. Any group of words that doesn't have a subject and verb is also a fragment.

Took an interest in astronomy (no subject).

Scott turning his telescope skyward every night (no adequate verb).

Although *ing* words look like verbs, no *ing* word by itself can ever be the verb of a sentence. It must have a helping verb in front of it.

Thinking about the big bang (no subject and no adequate verb).

To change these fragments into sentences, we must give each a subject and an adequate verb:

He took an interest in astronomy. (We added a subject.)
Scott was turning his telescope skyward every night. (We put a helping verb in front of the *ing* word to make an adequate verb.)
He was thinking about the big bang. (We added a subject and a helping verb.)

Sometimes we can simply tack a fragment onto the sentence before or after it.

Wondering why she had not come. I finally phoned her.
Wondering why she had not come, I finally phoned her.

Or we can change a word or two in the fragment and make it into a sentence.

I wondered why she had not come.

Are fragments ever permissible? Increasingly, fragments are being used in advertising and in other kinds of writing. In Exercise 3 you'll find advertisements that make use of fragments effectively to give a dramatic pause. But such fragments are used by professional writers who know what they're doing. The fragments are used intentionally, never in error. Until you're an experienced writer, stick with complete sentences. Especially in college writing, fragments should not be used.

EXERCISES

Put a period after each of the following that is a sentence. Make each fragment into a sentence either by adding an independent clause before or after it or by changing some words in it. Sometimes changing just one word will change a fragment into a sentence.

☐EXERCISE 1

1. After answering the telephone and taking the message

2. Having washed my only pair of jeans, I crawled into bed

3. After falling on the ice and breaking his leg

4. The announcement that there would be no classes on Friday

5. Perspiration is often more needed than inspiration

6. Whether I should continue my education

7. My parents wanting desperately to give me more than they had had

8. Not wanting to disappoint them

9. My father being a man of very decided opinions

10. Having always done his best in school

☐EXERCISE 2

1. Having walked through the forest all day without even a break for lunch

2. Where no person had ever set foot before

3. Trying to keep the fire burning

4. Weakened by lack of food and sleep, we were glad to go home

5. Having traveled almost two hundred miles

6. A boring evening in which we did nothing but watch TV

7. Not having anything to do all day but wait for the phone to ring

8. The gracious home that they had so carefully planned

9. A place where the puppy would feel secure

10. Finishing the day by vacuuming and doing the washing

Make each of the following into a smooth paragraph by getting rid of the fragments. Each of these particular fragments can be tacked onto the sentence before it. Simply cross out the period, and show that the capital letter should be a small letter by putting a diagonal line through it.

☐EXERCISE 3

Individuals can help save our forests. Americans waste vast amounts of paper. Because they don't think of paper as forests. They think nothing of wasting an envelope. Because an envelope is only a tiny piece of paper. But it takes two million trees to make the yearly supply of 112 billion envelopes. Even small savings can encourage others to save. Until finally the concerted efforts of enough individuals can make a difference.

Review of Run-Together Sentences and Fragments

SIX SENTENCES THAT SHOW HOW TO PUNCTUATE CLAUSES

I gave a party. Everybody came. I gave a party; everybody came.	(two independent clauses)
I gave a party; moreover, everybody came.	(two independent clauses connected by a word such as *also, consequently, finally, furthermore, however, likewise, moreover, nevertheless, otherwise, then, therefore, thus*)
I gave a party, and everybody came.	(two independent clauses connected by *and, but, for, or, nor, yet, so*)
When I gave a party, everybody came.	(dependent clause at beginning of sentence)
Everybody came when I gave a party.	(dependent clause at end of sentence) The dependent words are: *after, although, as, as if, because, before, even if, even though, ever since, how, if, in order that, since, so that, than, that, though, unless, until, what, whatever, when, whenever, where, whereas, wherever, whether, which, whichever, while, who, whom, whose, why.*

If you remember these six sentences and understand the rules for their punctuation, most of your punctuation problems will be taken care of. It is essential that you become familiar with the italicized words in the above table. If your instructor reads some of the words, be ready to tell which ones come between independent clauses and which ones introduce dependent clauses.

On a separate sheet rewrite these paragraphs making the necessary changes so there will be no run-together sentences or fragments.

1. The science of medicine has had a long history it began with superstitions and illness was attributed to evil spirits the ancient Egyptians were among the first to practice surgery anesthesia was, of course, unknown therefore the patient was made unconscious by a blow on the head with a mallet surgery was also practiced in early Babylonia and the Code of Hammurabi lists the penalties that an unsuccessful surgeon had to pay for example, if a patient lost an eye through poor surgery, the surgeon's hand was cut off.

2. In 1598 the famous Globe Theater was built across the Thames from London Shakespeare became a shareholder and his plays were produced there the theater was octagonal and held about twelve hundred people the "groundlings" stood on the floor and watched the play but the wealthier patrons sat in the two galleries those paying the highest fees could sit on the stage the stage jutted out into the audience thus the players and the audience had a close relationship.

USING STANDARD ENGLISH VERBS

This chapter and the next are for those who need practice in using standard English verbs. Many of us grew up speaking a dialect other than standard English, using phrases such as *I ain't, he don't, they was, I be, it do,* and *they has.* Such dialects are effective in their place, but in college and in the business and professional world, the use of standard English is essential. Frequently, though, after students have learned to speak and write standard English, they go back to their home communities and are able to slip back into their community dialects while they are there. Thus they have really become bilingual, able to use two languages—or at least two dialects.

The following tables compare four verbs in one of the community dialects with the same four verbs in standard English. Memorize the standard English forms of these important verbs. Most verbs have endings like the first verb *walk.* The other three verbs are irregular and are important because they are used not only as main verbs but also as helping verbs. We'll be using them as helping verbs in the next chapter.

Don't go on to the exercises until you have memorized the forms of these standard English verbs.

REGULAR VERB: WALK

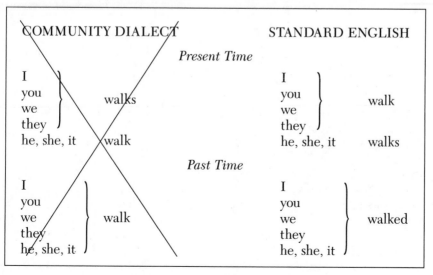

IRREGULAR VERB: HAVE

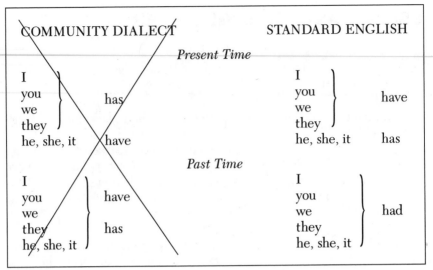

IRREGULAR VERB: BE

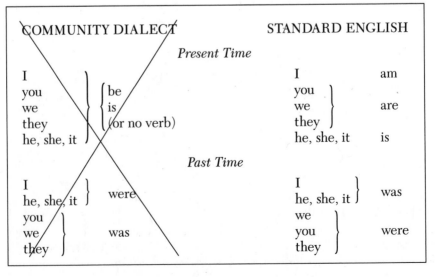

IRREGULAR VERB: DO

COMMUNITY DIALECT   STANDARD ENGLISH

Present Time

I
you
we   does
they
he, she, it   do

I
you
we   } do
they
he, she, it   does

Past Time

I
you
we   done
they
he, she, it

I
you
we   } did
they
he, she, it

Sometimes you may have difficulty with the correct endings of verbs because you don't hear the words correctly. As you listen to your instructor or to TV, note carefully the *s* sound and the *ed* sound at the end of words. Occasionally the *ed* is not clearly pronounced, as in *He asked me to go,* but most of the time you can hear it if you listen.

Try reading the following sentences aloud, making sure that you say every sound.

1. She seems to enjoy acting.
2. He likes to play golf and hopes to be a pro.
3. It costs too much to fly, so she drives.
4. He takes only a few minutes to eat a quick lunch.
5. I supposed they had already started.
6. He exposed the negative too long.
7. She's prejudiced against classical music.
8. I decided to rest before I started to study.

Now read some other sentences aloud from this text, making sure that you sound all the *s*'s and *ed*'s. Reading aloud and listening to others will help you use the correct verb endings automatically.

A good way to learn to speak standard English is to make a pact with a friend that you will both speak only standard English when you are together. By helping each other, you'll soon find yourselves speaking more easily.

EXERCISES

In these pairs of sentences, use the present form of the verb in the first sentence and the past form in the second. All the verbs follow the pattern of the regular verb *walk* except the three irregular verbs *have, be,* and *do.* Keep referring to the tables if you're not sure which form to use. Correct your answers for each exercise before going to the next.

☐EXERCISE 1

1. (walk) I often _____ to the park these days. I _____ in the park yesterday.

2. (be) I _____ happy now. I _____ not happy last week.

3. (have) She _____ a bike now. She _____ a moped last year.

4. (do) I _____ as I please now. I _____ as I pleased last year.

5. (need) He _____ help right now. He _____ help last fall.

6. (help) Her tutoring _____ me now. Her tutoring _____ me last semester.

7. (want) I _____ help right now. I _____ help yesterday.

8. (attend) He _____ a four-year college now. Last year he _____ a community college.

9. (talk) He _____ with her frequently now. He _____ with her last week.

10. (suppose) I _____ I'm late. They _____ that I had already gone.

☐EXERCISE 2

1. (be) I _____ tired now. I _____ tired last night too.

2. (do) I always _____ my best now. I _____ my best last year too.

3. (have) She _____ a scholarship now. She _____ a scholarship last year.

4. (ask) I _____ for help if I need it. I _____ for help last semester.

5. (enjoy) They _____ their garden now. They _____ their garden last summer.

6. (finish) She _____ work at two now. She _____ work at four last fall.

7. (learn) She _____ when she tries. She _____ a lot last year.

8. (work) He _____ hard these days. He _____ hard on his last job.

9. (listen) I _____ to her now. I _____ to her then.

10. (play) Now I _____ the drums. Last year I _____ the cello.

Underline the standard English verb form. All the verbs follow the pattern of the regular verb *walk* except the three irregular verbs *have, be,* and *do.* Keep referring to the tables if you are not sure which form to use.

□EXERCISE 3

1. I (join joined) the college orchestra last fall and (like likes) it.
2. I (play played) the drums in high school, but I (play plays) the flute now.
3. The orchestra director (need needs) more players and (hope hopes) to get some.
4. It (doesn't don't) matter whether one (be is) a music major.
5. We (work works) hard at each practice and (learn learns) a lot.
6. The director (expect expects) perfection and (insist insists) on it.
7. We (practice practices) two hours and then (has have) a short break.
8. Everyone (enjoy enjoys) those practices and (benefit benefits) from them.
9. We (watch watches) the director's baton and (do does) our best to follow.
10. Last night we (was were) pleased when the director (praise praised) us.

□EXERCISE 4

1. I never (like liked) English before, but now I (work works) hard at it.
2. Last week we (learn learned) about possessives and (discuss discussed) how to form them.
3. Our instructor (explain explained) what we (did done) wrong.
4. I (do does) my best in the course and (hope hopes) to pass.
5. Last semester I (like liked) the course in psychology, but I (drop dropped) chemistry.
6. I (check checked) into the requirements and (decide decided) not to major in math.

7. I (pick picked) this college because it (did done) well in football last fall.
8. The athletic coach (encourage encouraged) me to enroll, and I (listen listened) to his advice at that time.
9. Now when the going (get gets) rough, he always (be is) there.
10. He (advise advises) me and (treat treats) me like a friend.

In these sentences, cross out the community dialect expressions and write the standard English ones above.

☐EXERCISE 5

1. Last year our high school class travel to Washington, D.C.

2. Thirty of us and two teachers board the bus.

3. All of us was excited.

4. Before the trip, we learns about all the places to see.

5. I was surprise that the White House be on our tour.

6. I be glad to see it.

7. We has a half-hour tour through the Blue Room, the Red Room, the State Dining Room, and lots of other rooms.

8. We like the famous paintings of the presidents and first ladies.

9. We even walks past the place where Theodore Roosevelt's sons try to take their pony on an elevator.

10. All of us learn a lot on that trip.

JOURNAL WRITING

In your journal write about something that interests you at the moment using verbs you may formerly have had trouble with.

WRITING ASSIGNMENT

Continue with your writing assignments. Have someone dictate to you your list of spelling words on the inside back cover. Can you spell them all correctly now?

USING HELPING VERBS AND IRREGULAR VERBS

In the last chapter you studied the present and past forms of the regular verb *walk*. Other forms of regular verbs may be used with helping verbs. Here is a table showing all the forms of some regular verbs and the various helping verbs they are used with.

REGULAR VERBS

BASE FORM (Use after *can, may, shall will, could, might, should, would, must, do, does, did.*)	PRESENT	PAST	PAST PARTICIPLE (Use after *have, has, had.* Or use after some form of *be* to describe the subject.)	*ING* FORM (Use after some form of *be.*)
ask	ask *(s)*	asked	asked	asking
dance	dance *(s)*	danced	danced	dancing
decide	decided *(s)*	decided	decided	deciding
enjoy	enjoy *(s)*	enjoyed	enjoyed	enjoying
finish	finish *(es)*	finished	finished	finishing
happen	happen *(s)*	happened	happened	happening
learn	learn *(s)*	learned	learned	learning
like	like *(s)*	liked	liked	liking
need	need *(s)*	needed	needed	needing
open	open *(s)*	opened	opened	opening
start	start *(s)*	started	started	starting
suppose	suppose *(s)*	supposed	supposed	supposing
walk	walk *(s)*	walked	walked	walking
want	want *(s)*	wanted	wanted	wanting

Sometimes a past participle is used after some form of the verb *be* (or verbs that take the place of *be* like *appear, seem, look, feel, get, act, become*) to describe the subject.

He is satisfied.
He was confused.
He has been disappointed.
He appeared pleased. (He was pleased.)
He seems interested. (He is interested.)
He looked surprised. (He was surprised.)

He feels frightened. (He is frightened.)
He gets bored easily. (He is bored easily.)
He acts concerned. (He is concerned.)

Usually these past participles are called describing words that describe the subject rather than being called part of the verb of the sentence. What you call them doesn't matter. The only important thing is to be sure you use the correct form of the past participle (*ed* for regular verbs).

Note that when there are several helping verbs, it is the last one that determines which form of the main verb should be used: she *should* finish soon; she should *have* finished yesterday.

When do you write *ask, finish, suppose, use?* And when do you write *asked, finished, supposed, used?* Here's a rule that will help you decide.

Write *asked, finished, supposed, used*

1. When it's past time:

He *asked* her for a date last night.
She *finished* her paper yesterday.
When I saw you, I *supposed* you had had lunch.
I *used* to like her.

2. When some form of *be* (other than the word *be* itself) comes before the word:

She is *finished* with her paper now.
I am *supposed* to give you this note.
I am *used* to getting up early.

3. When some form of *have* comes before the word:

He has *asked* her to go out with him.
She had *finished* her paper last night.

IRREGULAR VERBS

All the verbs in the table on page 97 are regular. That is, they're all formed in the same way—with an *ed* ending on the past form and on the past participle. But many verbs are irregular. Their past and past participle forms change spelling instead of just adding an *ed.* Here's a table of some irregular verbs. (The present and the *ing* forms aren't usually given in a list of principal parts because they're formed easily from the base form and cause no trouble.) Refer to this list when you aren't sure which verb form to use. Memorize all the forms you don't know.

BASE FORM	PAST	PAST PARTICIPLE (use with a helper verb)
be	was, were	been
become	became	become
begin	began	begun
break	broke	broken
bring	brought	brought
buy	bought	bought
build	built	built
catch	caught	caught
choose	chose	chosen
come	came	come
cost	cost	cost
do	did	done
draw	drew	drawn
drink	drank	drunk
drive	drove	driven
eat	ate	eaten
fall	fell	fallen
feel	felt	felt
fight	fought	fought
find	found	found
fit	fitted *or* fit	fitted *or* fit
forget	forgot	forgotten *or* forgot
forgive	forgave	forgiven
freeze	froze	frozen
get	got	got *or* gotten
give	gave	given
go	went	gone
grow	grew	grown
have	had	had
hear	heard	heard
hold	held	held
hurt	hurt	hurt

BASE FORM	PAST	PAST PARTICIPLE (use with a helper verb)
keep	kept	kept
know	knew	known
lay (to place)	laid	laid
lead (rhymes with "bead")	led	led
leave	left	left
lie (to rest)	lay	lain
lose	lost	lost
make	made	made
meet	met	met
pay	paid	paid
read (pronounced "reed")	read (pronounced "red")	read (pronounced "red")
ride	rode	ridden
ring	rang	rung
rise	rose	risen
run	ran	run
say	said	said
see	saw	seen
sell	sold	sold
shake	shook	shaken
shine (to give light)	shone	shone
shine (to polish)	shined	shined
sing	sang	sung
sleep	slept	slept
speak	spoke	spoken
spend	spent	spent
stand	stood	stood
steal	stole	stolen
strike	struck	struck
swim	swam	swum
swing	swung	swung
take	took	taken
teach	taught	taught
tear	tore	torn
tell	told	told
think	thought	thought
throw	threw	thrown
try	tried	tried
wear	wore	worn
win	won	won
write	wrote	written

EXERCISES

Write the correct form of the verb. Refer to the tables and explanations on the preceding pages if you aren't sure which form to use after a certain helping verb. Do no more than ten sentences at a time before checking your answers.

☐EXERCISE 1

1. (finish) I should _____ my paper today, but I may not be _____ until tomorrow.

2. (finish) I could _____ in a few hours if I worked hard.

3. (finish) I have often _____ a paper rapidly, and I might _____ this one rapidly.

4. (finish) I am _____ it so that I can hand it in on Monday.

5. (finish) I wish that I had _____ it earlier.

6. (finish) It was _____ yesterday, but then I made some changes in it.

7. (finish) Now I must _____ it all over again.

8. (finish) When my paper is _____ , I'll be glad.

9. (finish) I always _____ whatever I start.

10. (finish) Most students have _____ their papers by now.

☐EXERCISE 2

1. (speak, begin) Newscasters always _____ standard English, and I now have _____ to imitate them.

2. (seem, want) That _____ to be a good way to learn standard English, and I now _____ to learn it.

3. (know, become) I _____ that it will help me in my job; in fact it has _____ a requirement in my field.

4. (imitate, use) I am _____ my teachers too because they all _____ standard English.

5. (teach, begin) I must _____ my ears to hear the standard endings of verbs, and I now am _____ to hear them.

6. (like) I _____ the feeling now of knowing two dialects.

7. (speak, learn) We had _____ to our son's teacher and had _____ that our son needs extra help.

8. (intend, begin) We now _____ to help him; in fact we _____ last night.

9. (be, realize) Last night as we _____ helping him, we _____ how much we can do.

10. (help, be, began) As we _____ him last night, we _____ impressed with how quickly he was _____ to catch on.

□EXERCISE 3

1. (be, see) We _____ delighted when we _____ our nephew's car turn into the driveway yesterday.

2. (see, begin) We hadn't _____ him for a year, and we had _____ to miss his visits.

3. (drive, eat) He had _____ five hundred miles that day and had _____ very little.

4. (offer, do) We _____ him some food immediately and _____ what we could to make him comfortable.

5. (eat, ask) He sat down then and _____ ravenously and _____ for more.

6. (write, ask, receive) Then he said he had _____ to us and _____ whether we had _____ his letter.

7. (come, begin) The letter hadn't _____, and we told him we had _____ to think he had forgotten us.

8. (see, suggest) We _____ that he was tired and _____ that he go to bed.

9. (go, wash, prepare) After he had _____ to bed, we _____ the dishes and _____ for the next day.

10. (see, be, drive) I _____ then that we _____ low on

food and _____ to the grocery store for more supplies.

□EXERCISE 4

1. (decide, see) Last winter I _____ to go to the annual ice carnival

at the college because I had never _____ one before.

2. (freeze, reach) I was almost _____ by the time I _____ the
rink.

3. (be, come) As I watched, however, I _____ glad I had _____ .

4. (observe, see) A friend of mine was competing in the figure skating,

and as I _____ her, I _____ that she was good.

5. (announce, win) Finally when the judges' decision was _____ ,

she had _____ first place.

6. (smile, receive) She _____ through her tears then as

she _____ the trophy.

7. (be, do) All her friends that night _____ pleased that she

had _____ so well.

8. (be, accept) _____ you there when she _____ her trophy?

9. (go, congratulate) That night we all _____ to a party

and _____ her.

10. (plan, intend) She now _____ to major in athletics and

_____ to teach figure skating.

AVOIDING DIALECT EXPRESSIONS

Although verbs cause the most trouble for those who have grown up speaking a dialect other than standard English, certain other expressions, more common in speech than in writing, should be avoided.

DIALECT	STANDARD ENGLISH
anywheres, nowheres, somewheres	anywhere, nowhere, somewhere
anyways	anyway
hisself, theirselves	himself, themselves
this here book, that there book, those there books	this book, that book, those books
them books	those books
he did good, she sang good	he did well, she sang well
my brother he plays ball	my brother plays ball
I be finished, she be finished, they be finished	I am finished, she is finished, they are finished
ain't	am not, isn't, aren't, hasn't, haven't

The following dialect expressions, called double negatives, should also be avoided.

DIALECT	STANDARD ENGLISH
haven't none, haven't got none	have none, haven't any
haven't no, haven't got no	have no, haven't any
haven't never	have never, haven't ever
haven't nothing	have nothing, haven't anything
wasn't no	was no, wasn't any
wasn't never	was never, wasn't ever
ain't got no	have no, haven't any

EXERCISES

Cross out the dialect expressions and write the standard English ones above.

☐EXERCISE 1

1. My sister she did good in the track meet last week.

2. I wasn't no good at sports, and anyways I ain't got time for them.

3. My brother he wasn't no expert at fixing cars.

4. He tried to fix his car hisself but he didn't know how to fix it good.

5. My uncle has a dog that ain't got no sense.

6. The dog runs somewheres, and then it don't come home.

7. I haven't never understood why my uncle has the dog.

8. But at least the dog be friendly.

9. This here book was assigned reading.

10. I be finished reading the book already.

☐EXERCISE 2

1. I walk somewheres every morning.

2. I haven't nothing else to do and anyways I like the exercise.

3. Anywheres I be going I prefer to walk.

4. After class my brother he always wants to stop somewheres for a snack.

5. I say I ain't got no money.

6. I tell him Mom she be fixing us something when we get home.

7. My mom be the best cook in town.

8. My parents be very generous with me.

9. When I started college last year, they bought me that there computer and them books.

10. Now that I make my own money, I haven't never asked for more help.

JOURNAL WRITING

Write three sentences using words you have used incorrectly in the exercises or in your papers.

Proofreading Exercise

See if you can correct the five errors in spelling and punctuation in this student paper. They are in the first and third paragraphs. You're on your own now. No answers are provided at the back of the book.

THE HAIRCUT

Like all college students, we were always broke. We constantly tried to save money in every way possible, and that lead to cutting out luxuries like barbers and hair stylists.

There we were—three guys with no money—all needing haircuts, so we agreed to cut each other's hair. I took first turn at doing the cutting on my not-too-confident friend while our third friend watched and provided encouragement.

It seemed like it should be easy but after about ten minutes with scissors and comb, it wasnt going well. In another five minutes of trying to correct my mistakes, it was even worse. The protests were growing and I managed only a few more snips before my friends insisted that I stop while their was any hair left. I must admit my handiwork looked terrible, and I suppose it was only natural that my offer to even it out a little was refused.

We pooled all our change and came up with just enough for one haircut—by a real barber—to fix up the damage I'd done.

Progress Test

This test covers everything you've studied so far. One sentence in each pair is correct. The other is incorrect. Read both sentences carefully before you decide. Then write the letter of the correct sentence in the blank.

_____ 1. A. It don't really matter to me whether you come or not.
       B. Your new suit is sharper than your old one.

_____ 2. A. I chose this course because I need it.
       B. I'm jogging every morning it's good exercise.

_____ 3. A. Thinking that I'd never pass that course.
       B. Don't you find your apartment too far from work?

_____ 4. A. Their trip into the city took two days.
       B. They was dissatisfied with the new ruling.

_____ 5. A. When my husband came home, he ask me where I'd been.
       B. What you think is important to me.

_____ 6. A. I've all ready finished writing my paper.
       B. It's the best one I've ever written.

_____ 7. A. If you can write a good paper, it's a help in college.
       B. I studied for four hours, then I went to bed.

_____ 8. A. I bought a new table; then I bought a rug.
       B. He seem happy when I saw him last night.

_____ 9. A. I'm taking a course of study that will lead to a degree.
       B. Wondering all the time how I'll make it through four years.

_____ 10. A. I'm surprise that you didn't get an A.
       B. I don't know whether to go to the play or to study.

_____ 11. A. I'd rather have a incomplete than a D in that course.
       B. Of course I'd rather have a C than either of them.

_____ 12. A. When I write my paper a week ahead then I can revise it.
       B. Revising is important for a good grade.

_____ 13. A. I invited her to go with me to see the play.
       B. I enjoyed the play however I was tired afterward.

_____ 14. A. Who's bike is that in our yard?
       B. I mowed the lawn and then settled down to study.

_____ 15. A. I hear that Brians car has faulty brakes.
       B. I'd advise him to get his brakes adjusted immediately.

MAKING SUBJECTS, VERBS, AND PRONOUNS AGREE

All parts of a sentence should agree. If the subject is singular, the verb should be singular; if the subject is plural, the verb should be plural.

Each of the boys has his own room.

Both have their own rooms.

He and I were there.

Many of the class were absent.

Some of the students were late.

The following words are singular and take a singular verb:

(*one* words)	(*body* words)	
one	anybody	each
anyone	everybody	either
everyone	nobody	neither
no one	somebody	
someone		

One of my friends is a freshman.

Everybody expects her to win.

Either of the girls is a good choice.

The following "group" words take a singular verb if you're thinking of the group as a whole, but they take a plural verb if you're thinking of the individuals in the group:

audience	dozen	herd	none
band	family	jury	public
class	flock	kind	team
committee	group	lot	
crowd	heap	number	

A dozen rolls *is* enough. . . . . A dozen *are* planning to go.
My family *is* behind me. . . . . My family *are* all scattered.
The jury *is* ready. . . . . The jury *are* still arguing.
The number present *was* small. . . . . . A number *are* going to the rally.

Here are some subject-verb pairs you can *always* be sure of. No exceptions!

you were	(*never* you was)
we were	(*never* we was)
they were	(*never* they was)
he doesn't	(*never* he don't)
she doesn't	(*never* she don't)
it doesn't	(*never* it don't)

Not only should subject and verb agree, but a pronoun also should agree with the word it refers to. If the word referred to is singular, the pronoun should be singular; if the word referred to is plural, the pronoun should be plural.

Each of the boys has *his* own car.

The pronoun *his* refers to the singular subject *Each* and therefore is singular.

Both of the boys have *their* own cars.

The pronoun *their* refers to the plural subject *Both* and therefore is plural.

Today many people try to avoid gender bias by writing sentences like the following:

If anyone wants a ride, he or she can go in my car.
If anybody calls, tell him or her that I've left.
Somebody has left his or her textbook here.

But those sentences are wordy and awkward. Therefore some people, especially in conversation, turn them into sentences that are not grammatically correct.

If anyone wants a ride, they can go in my car.
If anybody calls, tell them that I've left.
Somebody has left their textbook.

Such ungrammatical sentences, however, are not necessary. It just takes a little thought to revise each sentence so that it avoids gender bias and is also grammatically correct:

Anyone who wants a ride can go in my car.
Tell anybody who calls that I've left.
Somebody has left a textbook here.

Another good way to avoid the awkward *he or she* and *him or her* is to make the words plural. Instead of writing, "Each of the students was in his or her place," write, "All the students were in their places," thus avoiding gender bias and still having a grammatically correct sentence.

EXERCISES

Underline the correct word. Check your answers ten at a time.

☐EXERCISE 1

1. Everybody in our family (are is) planning a trip this summer.
2. Each of us (are is) going to a different part of the country.
3. One of my brothers (are is) going fishing in Wisconsin.
4. My other brother (doesn't don't) know yet where he'll go.
5. Each of them (are is) taking (his their) own motorcycle.
6. My sister and I (was were) planning to go to Virginia Beach.
7. Then my sister decided she (doesn't don't) want to go.
8. One of her friends (want wants) her to go to Dallas.
9. So my sister and her friend (think thinks) they'll go there.
10. My parents (intend intends) to drive to Tucson, Arizona, and I may go with them.

☐EXERCISE 2

1. Each of these rules (are is) important.
2. Doing the exercises (help helps) me remember the rules.
3. Some of the rules (are is) harder than others.
4. Each of the rules (has have) been a challenge to me.
5. A few of them (was were) familiar, but most of them (was were) new.
6. Every one of the rules (depend depends) on the previous rule.
7. It (doesn't don't) do any good to learn one isolated rule.
8. All of them (work works) together.
9. For example, the punctuation of sentences (require requires) a knowledge of subjects and verbs.
10. Each of the rules (are is) going to be of value in my writing.

☐EXERCISE 3

1. Everybody in our family (are is) going to the museum this afternoon.
2. Not one of us (has have) been there for ages.
3. All of us (feel feels) that we learn a lot every time we go.
4. One of my sisters (want wants) to see the exhibit of nineteenth-century costumes.

5. Both of my sisters (like likes) to design clothes.
6. Each of my brothers (has have) a special reason for going.
7. One of them (are is) collecting minerals and (want wants) to see the mineral collection.
8. My other brother (doesn't don't) want to miss the moon rock exhibit.
9. My parents just (follow follows) the rest of us around.
10. It (doesn't don't) take long for us to be ready for the museum lunchroom.

□EXERCISE 4

1. No one in our family (has have) ever been to Wind Cave National Park although all of us (has have) lived in South Dakota for years.
2. All of us (has have) talked about going to see it though.
3. Most of my friends (has have) visited it, and one of my friends (are is) going to visit it next week.
4. The stories about it (has have) intrigued us, and each of us (has have) a special reason for wanting to go.
5. One of my sisters (are is) now suggesting that we all go next month.
6. The main thing all of us (want wants) to do there is to take the mile-long guided tour through the various rooms in the cave.
7. The rooms (varies vary) in size from tiny boxlike rooms to a room the size of an auditorium.
8. Each of the rooms (has have) different formations on the walls such as boxwork, frostwork, and "popcorn" deposits.
9. One of my brothers (want wants) especially to see one of the prairie dog "towns" that (are is) common in the 44-square-mile park.
10. Each of my sisters (are is) interested in the desert plants such as the cactus and the yucca.

JOURNAL WRITING

Write about something that interests you using at least four words from your Spelling List on the inside back cover of this book.

CHOOSING THE RIGHT PRONOUN

Of the many kinds of pronouns, the following cause the most difficulty:

SUBJECT GROUP	NONSUBJECT GROUP
I	me
he	him
she	her
we	us
they	them

A pronoun in the Subject Group may be used in two ways:

1. As the subject of a verb:

He is my brother. (*He* is the subject of the verb *is.*)

He is taller than *I.* (The sentence is not written out in full. It means "He is taller than *I* am." *I* is the subject of the verb *am.*) Whenever you see *than* in a sentence, ask yourself whether a verb has been left off the end of the sentence. Add the verb, and then you'll automatically use the correct pronoun. In both speaking and writing, always add the verb. Instead of saying, "She's smarter than (I, me)," say, "She's smarter than I am." Then you can't fail to use the correct pronoun.

2. As a word that means the same as the subject:

That boy in the blue jeans is *he.* (*He* means the same as the subject *boy.* Therefore the pronoun from the Subject Group is used.)

It was *she* all right. (*She* means the same as the subject *It.* Therefore the pronoun from the Subject Group is used.)

Modern usage allows some exceptions to this rule however. *It is me* and *it is us* (instead of the grammatically correct *it is I* and *It is we*) are now established usage; and *it is him, it is her,* and *it is them* are widely used, particularly in informal speech.

Pronouns in the Nonsubject Group are used for all other purposes.

In the following sentence, *me* is not the subject, nor does it mean the same as the subject. Therefore it comes from the Nonsubject Group.

He came with Julie and *me.*

A good way to tell whether to use a pronoun from the Subject Group or the Nonsubject Group is to leave out the extra name. By leaving out *Julie,* you will say, *He came with me.* You would never say, *He came with I.*

We saw *him* and Loretta last night. (We saw *him* last night.)
He gave *us* boys a pony. (He gave *us* a pony.)
Dad asked Sis and *me* to wash the car. (Dad asked *me* to wash the car.)

EXERCISES

Underline the correct pronoun. Remember the trick of leaving out the extra name to help you decide which pronoun to use. Use the correct grammatical form even though an alternate form may be acceptable in conversation.

☐EXERCISE 1

1. It cost Dave and (I me) a dollar apiece to make that long-distance call.
2. It was worth it to both Dave and (I me) however.
3. We needed to know whether there were reservations for both (he and I, him and me).
4. We're going to a ski resort this weekend. It's the first time (he and I, me and him) have gone skiing.
5. We've worked hard this semester, and this will be a treat for (we us) both.
6. Dave is smarter than (I me), but he doesn't work as hard.
7. Consequently I usually get better grades than (he him).
8. This semester, though, (he and I, me and him) studied together.
9. No one could be better prepared for tomorrow's exam than Dave and (I me).
10. Maybe (he him) and (I me) will even get A's.

☐EXERCISE 2

1. Dad and (I me) promised Mom that we'd paint the back porch during my spring break.
2. It's not a big job for Dad and (I me); it's just been a problem to get at it.
3. It won't be the first painting job that (we us) two have done.
4. Last summer (he and I, him and me) painted the entire basement.
5. And two years ago (we us) two painted his car.
6. Mom and my sister do so many jobs around the house that it's really important for Dad and (I me) to do a bit too.

7. Mom keeps watching every day for Dad and (I me) to start, but we keep putting it off.
8. The trouble is that (he and I, him and me) never have the same free time.
9. Then yesterday Dad and (I me) did start the job, and before dark we had put on an entire first coat.
10. Mom said it was worth giving (we us) a special supper in the backyard.

□EXERCISE 3

1. Joan and (I me) are going on the choir tour in March.
2. It was a hard decision for (she and I, her and me) to make.
3. (She and I, Me and her) will miss an entire week of classes.
4. Both Joan and (I me) aren't exactly at the top of the class.
5. So missing a week's work may be hazardous for (we us).
6. (She and I, Me and her) will get a lot out of the trip though.
7. The choir director asked (we us) to pack the choir robes.
8. Both Joan and (I me) were pleased to be asked.
9. We're going all over the state to places neither Joan nor (I me) have ever been.
10. It's bound to be a great week for all of (we us) choir members.

□EXERCISE 4

1. (David and I, Me and David) have always been the best of friends.
2. There's always been a good feeling between (we us).
3. Last summer (he and I, me and him) took a trip to South Dakota.
4. It was the first long trip either David or (I me) had ever taken.
5. Time went very fast for David and (I me) on that trip.
6. (We Us) two shared the driving and drove long hours.
7. Sometimes in the evenings (he and I, me and him) had a game of chess.
8. It was always a close game between my friend and (I me).
9. (David and I, Me and David) had always wanted to see the Black Hills.
10. Seeing Mount Rushmore was a great experience for David and (I me).

MAKING THE PRONOUN REFER TO THE RIGHT WORD

When you write a sentence, *you* know what it means, but your reader may not. What does this sentence mean?

Joe told his father he would have to take the car to the garage.

Who would have to take the car? We don't know whether the pronoun *he* refers to Joe or to his father. One way to correct such a faulty reference is to use a direct quotation:

Joe said to his father, "I'll have to take the car to the garage."

Here's another sentence with a faulty reference:

I've always been interested in nursing and finally have decided to become one.

Decided to become a nursing? There's no word for *one* to refer to. We need to write

I've always been interested in nursing and finally have decided to become a nurse.

Another kind of faulty reference is a *which* clause that doesn't refer to any specific word.

No one could tell him where the bike had been left which made him angry.

Was he angry because no one could tell him or because the bike had not been left in its proper place? The sentence should read

It made him angry that the bike had not been left in its place.

or

It made him angry that no one could tell him where the bike had been left.

EXERCISES

Most—but not all—of these sentences aren't clear because we don't know what word the pronoun refers to. Revise such sentences, making the meaning clear. Remember that using a direct quotation is often the easiest way to clarify what a pronoun refers to. Since there are more ways than one to rewrite each sentence, yours may be as good as the one at the back of the book. Just ask yourself whether the meaning is clear.

□EXERCISE 1

1. I put the omelet on the table, took off my apron, and began to eat it.

2. They offered me a job which pleased me.

3. I've been trying to decide what trip to take which isn't easy.

4. She told her sister that her room was a mess.

5. I have a pair of glasses, but my eyes are so good that I don't use them except for reading.

6. The president told the dean he had been too lenient.

7. When I praised the child's finger painting, it was pleased.

8. I thought he would phone, and I waited all evening for it to ring.

9. The teachers arranged for a play center where they can play on swings, slides, and jungle gyms.

10. Felipe told the professor that his watch was wrong.

□EXERCISE 2

1. We couldn't find the cake plate and realized the children must have eaten it.

2. He told his dad he needed a new suit.

3. As I approached the baby's playpen, it began to cry.

4. When I moved the child's tricycle, it screamed.

5. After I read about Lindbergh's life, I decided that's what I want to be.

6. As soon as the fender was repaired, I drove it home.

7. I stopped at the old Wiley Schoolhouse, which has been designated a state historical site.

8. When I opened the door of the kennel, it ran away.

9. We couldn't find a single can of cola and blamed Rudy for drinking them.

10. His motorcycle swerved into the side of a house, but it wasn't damaged.

□EXERCISE 3

1. While I was holding the dog's water dish, it barked.

2. They offered me a job which pleased me.

3. I've been trying to decide what trip to take which isn't easy.

4. She told her sister that her room was a mess.

5. When Bob looked at his shoes he realized they didn't match.

6. Ellen told the riding instructor that her horse needed to be brushed.

7. When I tapped on the shark's aquarium, it swam away.

8. He told the lawyer about the case, which disappointed his parents.

9. I've always enjoyed painting and have decided to major in art.

10. Jill told her sister to call again when she wasn't so busy.

□EXERCISE 4

1. When I picked up the dog's dish, it began to whine.

2. I have been interested in coaching football ever since I was in high school, and now I have decided to become one.

3. I decided not to accept the summer job which annoyed my family.

4. She asked her sister why she wasn't invited to the party.

5. Jay's father let him take his new tennis racket to school.

6. I have always liked French Provincial furniture and have finally decided to buy one.

7. She told her instructor she didn't understand what she was saying.

8. She likes to swim; in fact she spends most of her summer doing it.

9. She is good in her studies although not very good in sports. This is why she was chosen student body president.

10. When the boss talked with Ed, he was really despondent.

□EXERCISE 5

1. Because I enjoy teaching I would like to be one.

2. My bicycle hit the car, but it wasn't damaged.

3. Fred told his cousin that his dog had ran away.

4. She was an excellent swimmer but couldn't run fast which is why she received the award.

5. The instructor told him his typewriter needed a new ribbon.

6. He told his father he ought to wash the car.

7. I walked into the room, climbed on the ladder, and began to paint it.

8. I'm taking lessons in golf, which is my favorite sport.

9. She told her mother she needed to be positive before making such a big decision.

10. Sarah told her sister that she needed to wash the car.

□EXERCISE 6

1. Andy told his brother that his car had a flat tire.

2. It would be cold in New England at this time of year which I don't like.

3. He asked the mechanic why he was having trouble.

4. When her sister came in at 4 A.M., she was crying.

5. As I tried to attach the dog's leash, it ran away.

6. Yesterday I turned in a paper that came back with an A grade.

7. The cars whizzed past, but they didn't even look my way.

8. As soon as I approached the robin's nest, it flew away.

9. I've decided to save all my money for a trip which won't be easy.

10. She told her daughter that she had missed her appointment.

□EXERCISE 7

1. As soon as the kitten's paw was bandaged, it ran off.

2. His brother said that he was a good tennis player.

3. She served me a pizza that was cold.

4. I learned the card trick which was easy.

5. I have adjusted the steering wheel, and you can take it home.

6. As Sam walked toward the coach, he was almost hit by a football.

7. He told the man to come back when he had time to talk.

8. When Jerome talked to his father, he was very angry.

9. Ben told his father he ought to get a refund for the faulty tire.

10. When I opened the door of the cage, it ran away.

CORRECTING MISPLACED OR DANGLING MODIFIERS

A modifier gives information about some word in a sentence, and it should be as close to that word as possible. In the following sentence the modifier is too far away from the word it modifies to make sense:

Chewing on an old shoe, we sat and watched the puppy.

Was it *we* who were chewing on an old shoe? That's what the sentence says because the modifier *Chewing on an old shoe* is next to *we*. It should be next to *puppy*.

We sat and watched the puppy chewing on an old shoe.

The next example has no word at all for the modifier to modify:

At the age of six my family moved to Bellevue, Washington.

Obviously the family was not six when it moved. The modifier *At the age of six* is dangling there with no word to attach itself to, no word for it to modify. We can get rid of the dangling modifier by turning it into a dependent clause.

When I was six, my family moved to Bellevue, Washington.

Here the clause has its own subject—*I*—and there's no chance of misunderstanding the sentence.

Here's another dangling modifier:

After a quick lunch, the bus left for Oakland.

Did the bus have a quick lunch? Who did?

After a quick lunch, I took the bus for Oakland.

EXERCISES

Most—but not all—of these sentences contain misplaced or dangling modifiers. Some you may correct simply by shifting the modifier so it will be next to the word it modifies. Others you'll need to rewrite. Since there is more than one way to correct each sentence, your way may be as good as the one at the back of the book.

□EXERCISE 1

1. While talking on the phone, the cake burned.

2. Sound asleep on the front porch, I came across my grandfather.

3. Crawling across the dusty road, I saw a furry little caterpillar.

4. Taking her in his arms, the moon hid behind a cloud.

5. You will enjoy looking at the pictures that you took years later.

6. By concentrating intently, I at last understood the paragraph.

7. Lincoln Park is the most interesting park in the city that I have seen.

8. She was engaged to a man with a Taurus named Victor.

9. At the age of fourteen my sister was born.

10. We gave all the food to the dog that we didn't want.

□EXERCISE 2

1. After cleaning my room, my dog wanted to go for a walk.

2. A son was born to Mr. and Mrs. N. L. Dixon weighing eight pounds.

3. Being a bore, I don't enjoy his company.

4. Except when picked, I don't care for cucumbers.

5. Screaming and kicking, I tried to quiet the child.

6. I bought a car from a used-car dealer with a leaky radiator.

7. Leaning against the barn, I saw the broken ladder.

8. After watching TV all evening, the dirty dishes were still on the table.

9. At the age of six my grandfather paid us a visit.

10. Slamming the door he marched out of the house.

□EXERCISE 3

1. While tobogganing down the hill, a huge bear came into view.

2. I saw a cute little rabbit on the way to school.

3. Dressed in a pink satin dinner dress, he thought she looked elegant.

4. Because of going to too many parties, my term paper was late.

5. We are having a series of lectures on religions of the world which will end May 30.

JOURNAL WRITING

Make up a sentence with a misplaced or dangling modifier, and then write the correction.

Proofreading Exercise

Can you find all ten errors in this student paper? No answers are provided.

I PRUNE A TREE

Are old cherry tree in the backyard had grown big and scraggly and I decided it needed pruning. I assumed of coarse that I could do the job easily because I'd often climbed the tree when I was a kid. In fact I had once built a tree house of sorts in it. So I got my saw, and started to climb. I learned a lot from that climb. First I learned that ants abound in trees they were everywhere. Second I learn that branches that look old and dead shouldn't be stepped on. I almost fell out of the tree learning that one. And finally I learned that its not easy to hold onto the tree with one hand while sawing with the other. I did it though, and before long I felt comfortable doing it. In fact I felt so comfortable that I did a little more pruning then I had originally intended to do. After quiet a while I decided to climb down and take a look at my work from the ground. . . .

Oh, Wow! Why didnt I call a tree expert!

USING PARALLEL CONSTRUCTION

Your writing will be clearer if you use parallel construction. That is, when you make any kind of list, put the items in similar form. If you write

He's good at skiing, skating, and plays basketball.

the sentence lacks parallel construction. The items don't all have the same form. But if you write

He's good at skiing, skating, and basketball.

then the items are parallel. They are all names of sports. Or you could write

He skis, skates, and plays basketball.

Again the sentence has parallel construction because the items all use the present form of the verb. Here are some more examples. Note how much easier it is to read the sentences with parallel construction.

LACKING PARALLEL CONSTRUCTION	HAVING PARALLEL CONSTRUCTION
She liked to work hard, to save her money, and then she would spend it all on a trip.	She liked to work hard, to save her money, and then to spend it all on a trip. (All three items start with *to* plus a verb.)
They were looking for a house with eight rooms, a two-car garage, and in a good location.	They were looking for a house with eight rooms, a two-car garage, and a good location. (All three items can be read smoothly after the preposition *with*.)
The interviewer wanted to know what college I had attended, whether I could use a word processor, and my experience.	The interviewer wanted to know what college I had attended, whether I could use a word processor, and what experience I had had. (All items are dependent clauses.)

The supporting points for a thesis statement (see p. 195) should always be parallel. For the following thesis statements, the supporting points in the left-hand column are not all constructed alike. Those in the right-hand column are; they are parallel.

NOT PARALLEL	**PARALLEL**
Belonging to a drama group was a good experience.	Belonging to a drama group was a good experience.
1. Dramatic training.	1. I got training in dramatics.
2. Speech improved.	2. I improved my enunciation.
3. Friendships.	3. I made good friends.
I've quit watching soaps.	I've quit watching soaps.
1. Wasting time.	1. Soaps wasted my time.
2. All the same.	2. Soaps are all the same.
3. Compared with reading.	3. Reading does more for me.

Using parallel construction will make your writing more effective. Note the effective parallelism in these well-known quotations:

Some books are to be tasted, others to be swallowed, and some few to be chewed and digested.

Francis Bacon

Let every nation know, whether it wishes us well or ill, that we shall pay any price, bear any burden, meet any hardship, support any friend, oppose any foe to assure the survival and success of liberty.

John F. Kennedy

Go back to Mississippi, go back to Alabama, go back to South Carolina, go back to Georgia, go back to Louisiana, go back to the slums and ghettos of our northern cities, knowing that somehow this situation can and will be changed.

Martin Luther King, Jr.

EXERCISES

Most—but not all—of these sentences lack parallel construction. Cross out the part that is not parallel and write the correction above.

☐EXERCISE 1

1. I like staying up late at night and to sleep late in the morning.

2. She taught her preschool son by reading to him, by teaching him songs, and she took him on neighborhood excursions.

3. Each student was given a choice of writing a term paper, taking a written exam, or an oral report could be given.

4. The driver warned us against littering, picking plants, or feeding the animals during our eight-hour drive through Denali National Park.

5. At the auction she bought a blender, two old chairs, and she also bought an old popcorn popper.

6. To create a beautiful room, it is more essential to have a knowledge of decorating than having a great deal of money.

7. They chose a house in the country because they wanted to grow their own vegetables, to give their children a country environment, and to enjoy the quiet of rural life.

8. Their house was on a lot 30 feet wide and 90 feet in depth.

9. The lecturer spoke with authority, illustrated his talk with personal incidents, and then concluded with a poem.

10. In this country we are promised the right to life, liberty, and the pursuit of happiness.

☐EXERCISE 2

1. Research shows that acidic pollutants cause widespread damage to paint, stone, wood, masonry, and they may even affect concrete and metals.

2. The Indian cliff dwellings in Mesa Verde National Park have been eroding slowly from the effect of brilliant sunlight, dusty winds, and stinging rain.

3. But the cliff dwellings may now be eroding more swiftly because nearby power plants emit pollutants that are carried to the cliff dwellings by wind, rain, or may even be carried by snow.

4. On our walk through the woods, we saw the buds on the maple trees opening, the tightly rolled leaves of the May apples showing their heads above ground, and the anemone blossoms were waving in the wind.

5. Some people say everything's good for something. They say even poisonous snake venom has value because medicines are being made from its enzymes to stop bleeding, to dissolve blood clots, and one medicine kills pain.

6. My brother says even old Christmas trees are good for something. He puts our old tree out in a snowdrift, makes sure its trunk is firmly on the ground, and then he decorates it with strings of raisins, apple bits, and popcorn, and sometimes he adds pinecones stuffed with suet.

7. It doesn't take long for the birds to find the feast and prove that our old Christmas tree is really good for something.

Make the supporting points of these thesis statements parallel.

□EXERCISE 3

1. Every college student should know how to type.
   1. Some instructors require typed papers.

   2. Saves time.

   3. Get higher grades.

2. Going home every weekend is unwise.
   1. I spend too much time on the bus.

   2. I get behind in my college work.

   3. Expensive.

   4. Miss out on weekend activities at college.

JOURNAL WRITING

Write two sentences with parallel construction, one telling the qualities you look for in a friend and the other telling your reasons for wanting a college education.

CORRECTING SHIFT IN TIME

If you begin writing a paper in past time, don't shift now and then to the present; and if you begin in the present, don't shift to the past. In the following paragraph the writer starts in the present and then shifts to the past.

> In *The Old Man and the Sea*, the Old Man has to fight not only the marlin and the sharks but also the doubts in his own mind. He wasn't sure that he still had the strength to subdue the giant marlin.

It should be all in the present:

> In *The Old Man and the Sea*, the Old Man has to fight not only the marlin and the sharks but also the doubts in his own mind. He isn't sure that he still has the strength to subdue the giant marlin.

Or it could be all in the past:

> In *The Old Man and the Sea,* the Old Man had to fight not only the marlin and the sharks but also the doubts in his own mind. He wasn't sure that he still had the strength to subdue the giant marlin.

The following paragraphs from student papers shift back and forth between past time and present. Change the verbs to agree with the time indicated by the first verb used, thus making the entire paragraph read smoothly.

□EXERCISE 1

That summer I decided to buy a radio receiver with the money I had earned mowing lawns. I set it up in my bedroom, and then I spent an afternoon getting an antenna on the roof. My mother stands down there on the lawn hollering advice at me because she's afraid I'm going to fall off the roof. In spite of her I finally get it up, and then I went inside and connected the antenna to the receiver. Presto! I am listening to radios all over the world. Eventually I decide I want a ham radio operator's license too so

I could transmit back to some of the stations I was hearing. I got the license all right, but being young and shy, I never did much talking. Mostly I just listen and work on my equipment. After a few months I tired of my new toy and never did any more with it. The challenge of striving for the set was more fun than actually having it.

□EXERCISE 2

I never knew anything about bloodhounds until a trainer talked to our law enforcement class last week. She said many people don't like bloodhounds because they aren't attractive with their loose flesh, drooping skin, and long leathery ears. Also, she says, they slobber so much that an excess of saliva often hangs down in ropes from their upper lips. But a bloodhound can often track a person that human searchers have failed to find. Bloodhounds can follow scents because they have as many as 105 cubic centimeters of olfactory membranes in their nostrils whereas humans have only about three cubic centimeters. She says people don't like to admit that even after bathing they smell, but they do. People can't recognize the smell, but a bloodhound can. Our bodies, she explained, shed skin at a rate of fifty million cells a day, and some of those cells are caught on grasses and shrubs, giving the bloodhound the scent.

□EXERCISE 3

Even though Robert Frost eventually became the most beloved of New England poets, his early career was not promising. After a few months in college, he decides that the routine of study is too much for him, and he became a bobbin boy in a mill. Later he married and once more tried college at Harvard but gave up after two years. Then followed a period in which he tramps, teaches school, makes shoes, and edits a weekly paper. Finally his grandfather took pity on him and bought him a farm. For eleven years he tried with scant success to wrest a living from the stony hills. During all this time he is writing poetry, but no magazine wanted it. Not until he sold his farm and went to England, where his first book of poems was published, did he become known. When he returned to America three years later, he finds himself famous.

JOURNAL WRITING

Write a brief paragraph describing an accident you once had. Then write another paragraph describing the same accident as if it's happening now.

CORRECTING SHIFT IN PERSON

You may write a paper in

> First person—*I, we*
> Second person—*you*
> Third person—*he, she, they, one, anyone, a person, people*

but don't shift from one group to another.

> Wrong: Few *people* get as much enjoyment out of music as *they* could. *One* need not be an accomplished musician to get some fun out of playing an instrument. Nor do *you* need to be very advanced before joining an amateur group of players.

> Right (but stilted): Few *people* get as much enjoyment out of music as *they* could. *One* need not be an accomplished musician to get some fun out of playing an instrument. Nor does *one* need to be very advanced before joining an amateur group of players.

(Too many *one*'s in a paragraph make it sound stilted and formal. Sentences can be revised to avoid using either *you* or *one*.)

> Better: Few *people* get as much enjoyment out of music as *they* could. It's not necessary to be an accomplished musician to get some fun out of playing an instrument. Nor is it necessary to be very advanced before joining an amateur group of players.

Often students write *you* in a paper when they don't really mean *you, the reader.*

You could tell that no one had been there in weeks.

Such sentences are always improved by getting rid of the *you.*

Obviously no one had been there in weeks.

Revise these student paragraphs so there will be no shift in person.

□EXERCISE 1

It is difficult to imagine life without telephones, but only a little over a hundred years ago there were no phones. In 1876 young Alexander Graham Bell invented the telephone. He had been working on a contraption to help his deaf students, and a wire went from his attic workshop to the basement where his helper Thomas Watson was working. Suddenly Watson picked up the end of the wire and heard Bell say, "Mr. Watson, come here. I want you." You can imagine how Watson rushed up the three flights of stairs, shouting "I can hear you! I can hear the words!" Bell's words were the first words ever spoken over a telephone wire.

□EXERCISE 2

The deer of the world have been growing a new set of antlers each year for about twenty million years. Antlers are shed in the winter and begin to grow again from buds called pedicels in the spring. The antlers are then protected by a distinctive skin called velvet, but by autumn the velvet begins to hang in tatters letting the antlers gleam. That antlers can regenerate is amazing. It's as if you cut off your arm and a new one grew.

□EXERCISE 3

Glaciers, I used to think, moved at a creeping pace, but now I've learned that Columbia Glacier, a forty-mile-long sheet of ice near Valdez, Alaska, traveled about ten feet a day one year. It's one of Alaska's largest glaciers and a popular tourist attraction. But if you compare that pace with the pace of Variegated Glacier at the head of the Alaska Panhandle, it's really slow. During part of 1982 and 1983 the Variegated Glacier surged forward at 180 feet a day. For that reason it was called "the galloping glacier."

☐**EXERCISE 4**

LIFE AFTER DEATH—OF A TREE

I always thought that if a tree died, it became unsightly and should be removed. Now I've learned differently. Of course you wouldn't really want a dead tree on your lawn, but in the forest a dead tree is of value. A standing dead tree provides nesting sites and shelter for birds and mammals such as owls, woodpeckers, chickadees, wrens, raccoons, and bears. Some eighty-five species of birds and forty-nine species of mammals make use of tree cavities. So, you see, a tree's life isn't over when it dies. Years later when it finally crashes to the ground and decomposes, you will find insects laying their eggs in its spongy wood. The insects are food for hungry mammals like the striped skunk, which likes the fat grubs it plucks from the rotting wood. Turtles and toads dig themselves into and under the fallen tree to hibernate. And finally some of the tree's nuts, which have been lying on the ground for years, find their way into the fertile soil of the rotting log and sprout into new saplings. The life of the tree goes on.

Adapted from *National Wildlife,* Aug.–Sept. 1985

☐**EXERCISE 5**

FREEDOM COSTS FREEDOM

I had worked all summer to save money for my first car. For months I'd kept at my job every day and saved every penny I earned. I'd never buy doughnuts at coffee break or dessert at lunch because every dollar saved brought me closer to the car I wanted so much. Finally for fifteen hundred dollars I bought a car that was just right for me.

A car is more than just a means of getting around. It's a status symbol. It's your sign of independence. It's your ticket to freedom. You don't have to ask to borrow the family car, and you don't have to explain where you are going or when you'll be back. Now I could drive where I wanted when I wanted.

The one thing I hadn't counted on, though, was how much it cost to keep a car running. With insurance, gas, and repairs, I found myself working just to support my car. My paychecks went for new wheel rims, car stereo components, and every accessory you could think of. I worked extra evenings to buy plush seat covers and overtime on weekends to buy new tires.

Funny how it costs so much of your freedom to support your freedom.

CORRECTING WORDINESS

Good writing is concise writing. Don't say something in ten words if you can say it as well, or better, in five. "In this day and age" isn't as effective as simply "today." "At this point in time" should be "at present" or "now."

Another kind of wordiness comes from saying something twice. There's no need to say "in the month of July" or "7 A.M. in the morning" or "my personal opinion." July *is* a month, 7 A.M. *is* morning, and my opinion *is* personal. All you need to say is "in July," "7 A.M.," and "my opinion."

Still another kind of wordiness comes from using expressions that add nothing to the meaning of the sentence. "The fact of the matter is that I'm tired" says no more than "I'm tired."

WORDY WRITING	CONCISE WRITING
an unexpected surprise	a surprise
as a general rule	as a rule
brown in color	brown
due to the fact that	because
each and every	each
enclosed herewith	enclosed
end result	result
fewer in number	fewer
free gift	gift
he was there in person	he was there
important essentials	essentials
in order to	to
in spite of the fact that	although
new innovation	innovation
past history	history
rectangular in shape	rectangular
refer back	refer
repeat again	repeat
serious crisis	crisis
small in size	small
ten pounds in weight	ten pounds
to my friend and myself	to my friend and me
two different kinds	two kinds
very unique	unique

EXERCISES

Cross out words or rewrite parts of each sentence to get rid of the wordiness. Doing these exercises can almost turn into a game to see how few words you can use without changing the meaning of the sentence.

☐EXERCISE 1

1. I woke up at 4 A.M. in the morning.

2. We were considering the question as to whether we should charge admission.

3. There are many people who never read a book from one end of the year to the other.

4. After our lengthy hike that lasted over eight hours, we were hungry for food.

5. He had tried several different sports. These sports included football, basketball, and hockey.

6. He is a man who can be depended upon to do what he says he will do.

7. I had an unexpected surprise yesterday when the guy who had roomed with me in college stopped in to see me.

8. I think, if I am not mistaken, that she is really planning to go.

9. I found that I had no money at all by the end of the year.

10. All of the three different kinds of stones we found were very unique.

☐EXERCISE 2

1. There is no doubt but that our team will win.

2. They carried him to his place of residence in an intoxicated condition.

3. At this point in time there is a lot more permissiveness than there used to be in years gone by.

4. In my personal opinion there is no doubt but that justice is too slow in this country of ours.

5. What I am trying to say is that in my opinion justice should be swift and sure.

6. Planning for the trip was left up to Mike and myself.

7. It is his height that makes him such a good basketball player.

8. The melons were large in size and sweet in taste.

9. The great percentage of students do not leave the campus on weekends.

10. The last point that I will try to make in this paper is the idea that one should learn more at college than just what is learned from one's courses.

□EXERCISE 3

1. It is my personal opinion that most people these days are spending entirely too much of their leisure time watching programs presented on TV.

2. The fact of the matter is that I completely forgot about the meeting that was scheduled for last night.

3. Most writers use too many words, repeating themselves and saying things over and over again.

4. When driving a new car for the first time, one must take care not to drive too fast for the first five hundred miles.

5. With reference to your letter, I may say that I really appreciate your kind invitation and am happy that I am able to accept.

6. What I intend to do is finish my year here and then look for a job that will bring in some money.

7. Most people, you will find, want a business form that is clear, concise, and easy to understand.

8. It seems to me that the president should take it upon herself to see that the motion comes to a vote of the members of the organization.

9. I couldn't help but think that she was just pretending to be ill.

10. I am making an effort to try to get rid of wordiness in my papers.

On a separate sheet rewrite this paragraph from a university publication, cutting its 124 words to about 53 and see how much more effective it will be.

□EXERCISE 4

One of the main problems of a student entering university is how to find his way around the many floors of the Library and how to use the materials. The students are confronted by rows of books, journals, complicated indexes, abstracts and ponderous reference works, and need help in finding the information they seek amid the mass of material. The Library staff recognizes its responsibility to help them utilize all this material. Orientation programs are given to all new students. Many faculty members bring their classes to a particular subject area or to the Government Publications for an orientation. Short printed handouts are available, such as special subject bibliographies, how to do computer searches, and how to use microfilm, periodical indexes, or psychological abstracts.

AVOIDING CLICHÉS

A cliché is an expression that has been used so often it has lost its originality and effectiveness. Whoever first said "light as a feather" had thought of an original way to express lightness, but today that expression is worn out. Most of us use an occasional cliché in speaking, but clichés have no place in writing. The good writer thinks up fresh new ways to express ideas.

Here are a few clichés. Add some more to the list.

all work and no play
apple of his eye
as luck would have it
bright and early
by the skin of our teeth
hard as nails
hungry as a bear
last straw
picture of health

pretty as a picture
proud as a peacock
roar like a lion
smooth as silk
spread like wildfire
strong as an ox
stubborn as a mule
wise as an owl

Clichés lack freshness because the reader always knows what's coming next. What comes next in these clichés?

birds of a . . .
bite off more than . . .
frightened out of . . .
heave a sigh of . . .
lend a helping . . .
odds and . . .
old as the . . .
raining cats and . . .

On a separate sheet rewrite these sentences to get rid of the clichés.

□EXERCISE 1

1. I hadn't cracked a book all weekend, so I decided to do a little studying before I hit the hay.
2. Then quick as a flash I had a better idea.
3. Studying is a pain in the neck, and I decided I'd rather dabble in the culinary art.

4. Therefore I went to the kitchen and slowly but surely got out all my equipment.
5. But as luck would have it, there were no eggs in the fridge and no cake mix in the cupboard.
6. I was at loose ends. You'd have died laughing if you'd seen me.
7. Since I couldn't find ingredients for anything, I decided to give the kitchen a cleaning to end all cleanings.
8. I worked like a dog and had everything clean as a whistle in no time at all.
9. But all good things must come to an end, and I finally decided that I'd better hit the books.
10. I studied that night until I was blue in the face, but the next morning I was up bright and early and all ready to ace that exam.

WRITING ASSIGNMENT

One way to become aware of clichés so you won't use them in your writing is to see how many you can purposely put into a paragraph. Write a paragraph describing your first morning on campus or on a job, using all the clichés possible while still keeping your account smooth and clear. You might start something like this: "I was up at the crack of dawn, fresh as a daisy, and raring to go. . . ." What title will you give your paper? Why a cliché of course! Writing such a paragraph should make you so aware of clichés that they'll never creep into your writing again.

Review of Sentence Structure

One sentence in each pair is correct. Read both sentences carefully before you decide. Then write the letter of the *correct* sentence in the blank. You may find any of these errors:

run-together sentence
fragment
wrong verb form
lack of agreement between subject and verb
wrong pronoun
faulty reference of pronoun
dangling modifier
lack of parallel construction
shift in time or person

_____ 1. A. Great Basin National Park in Nevada is our 49th national park it was dedicated in 1987.
   B. Samoa National Park was dedicated in 1988 and is our fiftieth national park.

_____ 2. A. The tutor helped both Renée and me.
   B. Hoping for a ride, the bus passed us by.

_____ 3. A. One of my friends is getting a job for the summer.
   B. I intended to study, but I watch a TV program instead.

_____ 4. A. Laughter is an indication of mental health some people never laugh.
   B. She had lost her camera but hoped she would find it.

_____ 5. A. If one wants a thrill, you should try waterskiing.
   B. Our team won the first game but lost in the finals.

_____ 6. A. We was planning a get-together after the game.
   B. I worked for hours but didn't get my paper finished.

_____ 7. A. Each of my sisters has her own car now.
   B. Getting that A pleases me and gave me new confidence.

_____ 8. A. He had worked as a farmhand, a chauffeur, and in a mine.
   B. That sports car belongs to my fiancé and me.

_____ 9. A. Hoping for years that I could go to college and then finally making it.
   B. I liked his good humor, his easygoing way, and his generosity.

_____ 10. A. He was surprise to hear from her.
   B. They invited my boyfriend and me to their cottage.

_____ 11. A. The professor told my friend and I that we had passed.
        B. One of us is making a mistake.

_____ 12. A. Each of the candidates is well qualified for the job.
        B. Bright red and steaming, I took the lobster from the boiling water.

_____ 13. A. The group leader asked my friend and me to canvass our block.
        B. Because he wanted people he could depend on.

_____ 14. A. He told the supervisor he had made a mistake.
        B. We freshmen were entertained by the upperclassmen.

_____ 15. A. They invited Diane and me to dinner.
        B. An invitation which of course pleased us.

_____ 16. A. He mowed the lawn, trimmed the hedge, and then he pruned the bushes.
        B. Drive carefully.

_____ 17. A. When I entered the cottage, you could see that someone had been there.
        B. I've finished mowing the lawn and now am going to rest.

_____ 18. A. The president asked Karen and me to be on the nominating committee.
        B. I can't decide whether to become a teacher, a secretary, or go into social work.

_____ 19. A. Having finished all my homework, I went to bed.
        B. He told his dad that his car needed a tune-up.

_____ 20. A. Every one of my plants are withering.
        B. They expected us students to keep our rooms tidy.

_____ 21. A. One of my cousins is getting married in the spring.
        B. Which is what we had been expecting her to do.

_____ 22. A. Running to catch the bus, she slipped and fell.
        B. I had finish my paper before it was due.

_____ 23. A. Because most of us intend to get jobs during vacation.
        B. Having finished play practice, they went out for some food.

_____ 24. A. I rewrote my paper, typed it, proofread it, and ran for class.
        B. He always comes late therefore he often misses the assignment.

_____ 25. A. You can improve your vocabulary it just takes determination.
        B. Winning that trophy was the best thing that ever happened to him.

Proofreading Exercise

Can you find the seven errors? No answers are provided.

TO THE POLE

In the spring of 1986 seven men and one woman started to walk to the North Pole. Their intention was to make the trek without outside assistance. No food or supplies were flown in to them and no information was given to them by radio concerning there geographic position. They depended entirely on their sextant and chronometer to guide them, and they loaded 1,350 pounds of food and equipment on each of their five sleds pulled by their dogs.

At first the sleds were to heavy to maneuver across the rough ice, and it was necessary to go back and forth with partial loads for the first few weeks. As a result, they traveled three miles for every mile they went forward. Some of the time it was −68°F.

As they ate the food the loads became lighter, and they trimmed the sleds down by cutting off some of the wood and burning it for heat. Eventually a entire sled was eliminated, and the dogs that had pulled it were airlifted back to civilization. Also two members of the group were airlifted out because of illness thus the group finally consisted of five men, a women, twenty-one dogs, and barely enough food to last.

But the six of them, in spite of a number of near catastrophes, were determined to reach the Pole through their own power and perseverance. They walked about 1,000 miles, which was twice the straight-line distance of 478 miles. And reach the Pole they did on May 2. They were the first group to walk to the Pole without resupply since Peary's expedition in 1909. And Ann Bancroft, a 30-year-old schoolteacher from Minnesota, was the first woman ever to walk to the Pole.

Punctuation and Capital Letters

3

3 Punctuation and Capital Letters

PERIOD, QUESTION MARK, EXCLAMATION MARK, SEMICOLON, COLON, DASH

Every mark of punctuation should help the reader. Just like red and green signals at an intersection, marks of punctuation will keep the reader, like the traffic, from getting snarled up.

Here are the rules for six marks of punctuation. The first three you have known for a long time and have no trouble with. The one about semicolons you learned when you studied independent clauses (p. 69). The ones about the colon and the dash may be less familiar.

Put a period at the end of a sentence and after most abbreviations.

Mr.	A.D.	Dr.	Wed.	sq. ft.
Ms.	etc.	Jan.	P.M.	lbs.

Put a question mark after a direct question (but not after an indirect one).

Shall we go? (the exact words of the speaker)
He asked whether we should go. (not the exact words of the speaker)

Put an exclamation mark after an expression that shows strong emotion. Use it sparingly.

Great! You're just in time!

Put a semicolon between two closely related independent clauses unless they are joined by one of the connecting words *and, but, for, or, nor, yet, so.* (Refer to p. 70 to review the semicolon.)

> The rain came down in torrents; we ran for shelter.
> I have work to do; therefore I must leave.

Actually you can write acceptably without ever using semicolons because a period and capital letter can always be used instead of a semicolon.

> The rain came down in torrents. We ran for shelter.
> I have work to do. Therefore I must leave.

Put a colon after a complete statement when a list or long quotation follows.

> We took the following items: hot dogs, potato chips, and coffee. (*We took the following items* is a complete statement. You can hear your voice fall at the end of it. Therefore we put a colon after it before adding the list.)
>
> We took hot dogs, potato chips, and coffee. (Here *We took* is not a complete statement; it needs the list to make it complete. Therefore, since we don't want to separate the list from the first part of the sentence, no colon is used.)
>
> The speaker closed with a quotation from Emerson: "The only true gift is a portion of thyself." (*The speaker closed with a quotation from Emerson* is a complete statement. Therefore we put a colon after it before adding the quotation.)
>
> Emerson said, "The only true gift is a portion of thyself." (*Emerson said* is not a complete statement. Therefore we don't put a colon after it.)

Use a dash to indicate an abrupt change of thought or to throw emphasis upon what follows. Use it sparingly.

> A mother's role is to deliver children—by labor once and by car forever after.

EXERCISES

Add to these sentences the necessary punctuation (period, question mark, exclamation mark, semicolon, colon, dash). Not all sentences require additional punctuation. Also, your answer may differ from the one at the back of the book because either a semicolon or a period with a capital letter may be used between two independent clauses.

☐EXERCISE 1

1. We ran for the bus we almost missed it.
2. Finally we got on with all our equipment skis, tote bags, boots.
3. Luckily we hadn't brought any suitcases, garment bags, or other gear.
4. It was an hour's trip to Lake Placid we'd never been there before.
5. The scenery along the way was beautiful we didn't miss a thing.
6. Soon we were there the place surpassed all our expectations.
7. The snow was deep and crusty it was a perfect day for skiing.
8. That was the beginning of a good week I'll never forget it.
9. I couldn't decide what I liked best the skiing, the scenery, or the food.
10. That was only the first of our trips to Lake Placid it made us want more.

☐EXERCISE 2

1. Henry Ford built his car in a shed behind his home, using the following materials scrap metal, four bicycle wheels, and a doorbell for a horn.
2. Then one night he was ready to try it out he was too excited, however, to wait until morning.
3. At three A.M. he cranked it and rode out of the shed America has never been the same since.
4. In 1908 his first Model T appeared by 1913 he was turning out over two hundred thousand Model T's a year.
5. A Model T cost $290 in 1924 a comparable Ford today would cost about $20,000.
6. By 1930 there were twenty-three million cars on the road in the United States that was one for every five people.
7. For years the U.S. auto companies had little competition then came the gasoline shortage.
8. People turned from the big gas guzzlers to the compacts American companies could not keep up.
9. The Japanese could because they had three advantages more efficiently operated plants, teamwork between labor and management, and devoted employees.
10. American companies learned from the Japanese therefore they finally made a comeback.

□EXERCISE 3

1. Have you ever been to Greenfield Village in Dearborn, Michigan.
2. It's not only a reconstructed historical village it's almost an autobiography of Henry Ford.
3. In his early years Ford wasn't interested in the past then in 1919 he began to reconstruct the old Ford family farm.
4. Later he moved the buildings to Dearborn then he began to add other buildings.
5. He reconstructed the shop where he had built his first horseless carriage next he added the first factory of the Ford Motor Company.
6. No expense was too great he spent half a million dollars, for example, to restore an old country inn.
7. The 107 houses and shops in the village span three hundred years of American history and include a toy store, drugstore, barbershop, baker's shop, milliner's shop, and locksmith's shop.
8. Ford scoured the country to find furniture and china to refurnish the buildings he wanted an example of every article that had been used in America from the days of the first settlers to his own day.
9. Nothing was too small or insignificant for his museum one collection, for example, shows the evolution of the clothespin.
10. His Model T Ford had just about abolished the old way of life Ford tried, however, to reconstruct that way of life in Greenfield Village.

□EXERCISE 4

1. I thought there had always been pencils now I've learned that the United States has had pencils only since 1827.
2. During the Middle Ages paper was marked with ink by using a brush called a *penicillus,* a Latin word meaning "little tail" from that word has come our word *pencil.*
3. In 1564 in England an unusually pure deposit of graphite was discovered people found they could make marks on paper with it.
4. They cut the graphite into rods and wrapped the rods with twine then they unwound the twine from one end as needed in writing.
5. In 1662 a graphite pencil was made in Nürnberg, Germany, it was the first pencil ever made.
6. Napoleon then commissioned a man named Conté to develop a substitute for the imported German pencils Conté in 1793 was issued a patent for his process.
7. He mixed clay with graphite and water and pressed the paste into grooves in cedarwood to dry his process was the forerunner of modern pencils.

8. In the United States the first pencils were manufactured in Salem, Massachusetts, in 1827 now over two billion pencils are sold in the United States annually.
9. Yellow has always been the favorite color for pencils pencils in any other color simply do not sell.
10. Today we write with pencils without thinking of their long history.

☐EXERCISE 5

1. Terry Fox was an outstanding Canadian soccer and basketball player then he lost his right leg to cancer.
2. But he refused to give up he decided to run a "marathon of hope" across Canada to aid cancer research.
3. He started in Newfoundland in April 1980 his goal was to finish in Vancouver.
4. Terry ran with a kind of hop and skip on his artificial leg some days he ran as much as thirty miles.
5. He endured all kinds of weather rain, snow, hailstones, and blistering heat.
6. Everyone admired his pluck and perseverance they came out to see him and to give him money or pledges.
7. In Toronto ten thousand people greeted him he had become a national hero.
8. Then in September, halfway across Canada, he had to give up the disease had spread to his lungs.
9. In four and a half months he had run 3,317 miles furthermore he had collected over twenty million dollars for the Canadian Cancer Society.
10. And he had made his point "I wanted to show people," he said, "that just because they're disabled, it's not the end."

☐EXERCISE 6

1. Why is the U.S. so slow in adopting metric.
2. Metric is used by every nation in the world except three Burma, Liberia, and the U.S.
3. How did the system we use get started.
4. Our system started years ago when Britain said a yard was the distance from the nose of King Henry I to the tip of his middle finger.
5. Yet Britain changed to metric in the early 1970s Canada followed in 1977.
6. In Canada speed limits are posted in kilometers gas is measured in liters.
7. Americans resist change in a 1977 Gallup Poll more than two-thirds of those polled were against changing to metric.

8. Now, however, there are hopeful signs industry is finding it almost impossible to sell nonmetric goods abroad.
9. For example, in 1989 General Electric sent a shipment of appliances to Saudi Arabia the shipment was rejected because the connecting cords were 6 feet long instead of the required 2 meters (6.6 feet).
10. Metric is the worldwide standard system the U.S. cannot afford to lose its place in the global economy.

□EXERCISE 7

1. Did you know that horses are making a comeback on farms.
2. For years horses were considered an outmoded source of energy now they are the latest thing.
3. On many farms giant draft horses are being used for the following jobs planting, plowing, mowing, and hay loading.
4. Horses don't compact the soil thus they are better in that way than tractors.
5. They have no trouble starting on a cold morning tractors sometimes do.
6. They will work for fifteen or twenty years the life of a tractor is about half that.
7. Horses are a source of power that reproduces itself other kinds of power deplete the source.
8. Of course the main advantage of horses is that they are fueled by homegrown food furthermore they add fertilizer to the soil.
9. It is true that a tractor can move more than three times as many logs in a day as horses can however the horses don't tear up tree roots or skin away the bark of other trees.
10. Horses will never take the place of tractors on huge farms they are useful, however, as an alternate energy source for smaller jobs.

□EXERCISE 8

1. Quite a few large corporations have switched to metric even some government agencies, including NASA, have converted.
2. In 1973 General Motors began building metric cars (everything except the speedometers) Ford and Chrysler followed.
3. Most companies now maintain dual systems yards and ounces for goods sold in the U.S. and metric for exports.
4. In 1989 more than 60 percent of major corporations manufactured at least some metric products they of course had to maintain dual systems.
5. Maintaining dual systems is expensive and complicated soon the dual systems will have to go.

6. Business is leading the way social and cultural changes will follow.
7. The Olympics in Los Angeles in 1984 were run entirely in metric it will probably set a trend for other athletic events.
8. The national parks now use both miles and kilometers on their signs because tourists come from many countries.
9. More than half the states now require metric instruction in the schools the next generation will thus not have metric phobia.
10. Soon the new generation will take over management then they will bring the U.S. into line with the rest of the world.

Source: *U.S. News and World Report,* March 1990

JOURNAL WRITING

Write two sentences that list the things you want to buy on your next shopping trip. Structure the first sentence with a colon and the second without a colon.

Proofreading Exercise

Can you find the five errors in this paragraph? No answers are provided.

RECYCLING

As landfill capacity dwindles recycling is becoming the prudent choice for local governments ten states now have mandatory recycling programs, and more then six hundred communities have some type of curbside recycling in which residents sort certain recyclable materials such as aluminum and newspapers. Leaders among large cities include San Jose and Seattle each boasts a nearly 60 percent participation rate. Top honors probably go to Hamburg, New York, where 90 percent of the three thousand households recycle there trash.

Source: *National Wildlife,* Feb.–Mar. 1989

COMMAS (RULES 1, 2, AND 3)

Students often sprinkle commas through their papers as if they were shaking pepper out of a pepper shaker. Don't use a comma unless you know a rule for it. Commas are important because they prevent the reader from misreading the sentence.

You need only six comma rules. MASTER THESE SIX RULES, and your writing will be easier to read. You have already learned the first rule on page 70.

1. **Put a comma before *and, but, for, or, nor, yet, so* when they connect two independent clauses.**

   He found a ten dollar bill, and that was the end of his studying.
   I may try to get a new job, or I may stick with this one.
   I like him, but I don't want to marry him.
   I love her, so I am planning to marry her.

Be sure such words do connect two independent clauses. The following sentence is merely one independent clause with one subject and two verbs. Therefore no comma should be used.

   She wanted to go to college but didn't have enough money.

2. **Put a comma between three or more items in a series.**

   He ordered pie, cake, and ice cream.
   She slammed the door, ran down the walk, and got in her car.

Some words "go together" and don't need a comma between them even though they do make up a series.

   He wore a baggy old red sweater.
   The bright blue morning sky gave her a lift.

The way to tell whether a comma is needed between two words in a series is to see whether *and* could be used naturally between them. It would sound all right to say *pie and cake and ice cream;* therefore commas are used. But it would not sound right to say *baggy and old and red sweater* or *bright and blue and morning sky;* therefore no commas are used. Simply put a comma where an *and* would sound right.

It's permissible to omit the comma before the *and* connecting the last two items of a series, but more often the comma is used.

If an address or date is used in a sentence, treat it as a series, putting a comma after every item, including the last.

He was born on May 17, 1972, in Mesa, Arizona, and grew up there.
She lived in Pleasant Hill, California, for two years.

When only the month and year are used in a date, the commas are omitted.

In May 1980 he moved to Zanesville, Ohio.

3. **Put a comma after an introductory expression that doesn't flow smoothly into the sentence, or before an afterthought that is tacked on at the end.** It may be a word, a group of words, or a dependent clause.

Yes, I'll go.
Well, that was the end of that.
Moreover, the umpire agreed with me.
Running down the hill, she slipped and fell.
It's cold this morning, isn't it?
When you have finished, your dinner will be ready.

When you studied dependent clauses, you learned that a dependent clause at the beginning of a sentence needs a comma after it. In the last example above, you can see that a comma is necessary. Otherwise the reader would read *When you have finished your dinner* before realizing this was not what the writer meant. A comma prevents misreading.

EXERCISES

Punctuate these sentences according to the first three comma rules.

☐EXERCISE 1

1. When I am going on a trip I plan long in advance.
2. I read travel brochures and I make lists of what I want to see.
3. If I have time I consult books in the library.
4. I also look at newspapers encyclopedias and travel magazines.
5. Yes planning is half the fun of travel isn't it?

6. Even if I'm not going far away the planning is enjoyable.
7. When I've done a lot of planning the entire trip goes more smoothly.
8. After I finish college I intend to take a really long trip.
9. I might go to Hawaii Tahiti or Australia.
10. Even if I don't go that far it's fun to think about it.

□EXERCISE 2

1. I've been having trouble concentrating lately and I have to do something about it.
2. Since I've been out of school for several years it's difficult to get back in the swing.
3. Although my professors aren't dull my mind still wanders.
4. I'll be listening to an interesting lecture and then suddenly my mind is miles away.
5. Just a word can ensnare me and I'm off.
6. Since I've got to quit this daydreaming I'm trying a new plan.
7. Whenever my mind drifts off I put down a mark on a sheet of paper.
8. Then I yank my mind back and concentrate for a while.
9. At the end of every period I have a lot of marks but each day they become fewer.
10. One of these days I'll have no marks at all and then I'll have reached my goal.

□EXERCISE 3

1. More than any other animal the bison is a symbol of the West.
2. Nearly wiped out in the 1800s the bison are now making a comeback.
3. When Lewis and Clark explored the West there were about sixty million bison.
4. But in the 1800s they were slaughtered by the settlers by sportsmen and by hide and meat hunters.
5. Hoping to subdue the Indians by cutting off their food supply the U.S. Army also slaughtered the bison.
6. By 1889 only 551 bison were alive in the United States and of those a herd of twenty was almost wiped out by poachers.
7. Under careful management the bison have now made a comeback and there are at present about seventy-five thousand in the United States.
8. They are kept in preserves such as Yellowstone National Park National Bison Range in Montana and Theodore Roosevelt National Park in North Dakota.
9. Although the bison are not completely free they're given adequate space to roam.
10. These shaggy beasts are part of our national heritage and they must be helped to survive.

☐EXERCISE 4

1. Of the fifty-four national parks in the United States only seven are in the East.
2. They are Acadia in Maine Shenandoah in Virginia Mammoth Cave in Kentucky Great Smokey Mountains in Tennessee and North Carolina and the Everglades Biscayne and Dry Tortugas in Florida.
3. Perhaps the best known is Mammoth Cave in Kentucky.
4. When I was in the South last summer I decided to visit Mammoth Cave.
5. I had read about stalactites and stalagmites but I was not prepared for their amazing variety.
6. A stalactite projects downward from the ceiling of the cave and a stalagmite projects upward from the floor.
7. Both are formed by the dripping of mineral-rich water and both have taken many years to form.
8. Some are tinted with manganese or iron oxide and have a purple brown or reddish tint.
9. While I was in the cave I also saw gypsum and crystal formations in the shapes of flowers.
10. Mammoth Cave has the longest recorded cave system in the world with 300 miles of passages on five levels and I walked along a few of the passages.

☐EXERCISE 5

1. Some of the most striking formations in Mammoth Cave are Crystal River Frozen Niagara and Cathedral Domes.
2. Before I left I took a boat ride on the underground Echo River.
3. Now I want to see more national parks for they include the most striking natural scenery of our country.
4. Our national parks cover some 80 million acres and they have about 273 million visitors a year.
5. Yellowstone was the first national park to be created and no other park the same size has as many natural wonders.
6. In Yellowstone are geysers hot springs lakes rivers and cataracts.
7. Of the two hundred active geysers in Yellowstone Old Faithful is the most famous.
8. Ever since it was discovered in 1870 it has been spouting on an average of every sixty-five minutes.
9. Since the intent of national parks is to preserve the balance of nature animal and plant life are disturbed as little as possible.
10. Hunting and lumbering are prohibited but fishing is allowed.

☐EXERCISE 6

1. With a galloping speed of up to thirty-five miles an hour the giraffe is one of the swiftest animals.
2. The Arabs called it *zarafa* or "swift creature" and thus it got its name.
3. Few animals are so delicate yet giraffes have survived for twenty-five million years.
4. Of the 400,000 giraffes that exist today most are in East Africa.
5. Of those that have been measured the tallest was 19 feet 3 inches.
6. Since a giraffe's eyes are set in sockets bulging from its head the giraffe has almost 360-degree vision.
7. Each giraffe may eat one hundred pounds of leaves twigs and branches in a day.
8. The giraffe curls its 1½-foot tongue around a branch draws it between its thick lips and skims off a mouthful of twigs.
9. Its favorite tree is the acacia and some acacia seeds won't take root unless they've been through a giraffe's digestive system.
10. The female giraffe gives birth while standing and drops her calf five or six feet to the grass.

☐EXERCISE 7

1. Since giraffes do little harm they are likely to survive.
2. They seldom molest anyone and they don't kill people as lions do.
3. They won't bend down for the grass that sheep and cattle eat and they don't trample crops as elephants do.
4. Among the most graceful of animals the giraffe adds to the interest of the African countryside.
5. In national parks throughout the world the feeding of wild animals is forbidden.
6. But the law is often ignored and people feed wild animals potato chips bread cheese and just about anything.
7. Even though signs warn that such food is not good for animals the public cannot resist giving handouts.
8. The animals are thus lured to the highways and may be struck by cars.
9. Since there are never enough wardens to enforce the antifeeding laws hundreds of animals are killed in this way each year.
10. Through thoughtlessness the public is depleting the number of animals in national parks.

☐EXERCISE 8

1. When Phil Mahre won his third World Cup in skiing he didn't even seem excited.
2. He says he just skis for the fun of it and he thinks about the Cup later.

3. He was the first American ever to win a World Cup in skiing and now he has won three.
4. He excels in three skiing disciplines: slalom giant slalom and downhill.
5. Phil and his twin brother, Steve, are among the best skiers in the United States and they've always been competitors.
6. Sometimes Phil will win a race by a second or two and sometimes it will be Steve.
7. Steve was born four minutes after Phil and says that he's been trying to catch up ever since.
8. They used to time each other with stopwatches and try to improve their techniques.
9. Both have had broken bones to cope with but both have had the resilience to come back.
10. Instead of being tense or ambitious they both laugh and say that games are for fun.

□EXERCISE 9

1. Until I read a recent article I didn't know what a California condor was.
2. Now I know it's the largest bird in North America with a wingspan of nine feet and I know that hundreds of condors used to live along the West Coast from Mexico to California.
3. Today not a single condor can be seen in the wild and only a few are in captivity.
4. Because the birds were close to extinction scientists decided to capture the few remaining birds.
5. They hoped they might save the species and in 1987 they caught the last condor in the wild.
6. By then only twenty-seven condors existed and if they hadn't been captured the species would certainly have become extinct.
7. Condors had neared extinction for several reasons. First human populations had taken over their habitats.
8. Second condors often ate the discarded remains of animals shot by hunters and from those remains they swallowed bullets or shotgun pellets and thus died of lead poisoning.
9. Third before protective laws were passed people often shot condors thoughtlessly.
10. Now several thousand acres have been set aside in California as condor habitat and public concern for the birds is growing.

☐**EXERCISE 10**

1. The scientists at the San Diego Wild Animal Park hoped the twenty-seven condors would produce young and eventually condors could be returned to the wild.
2. Because the scientists feared that the condors might break the eggs in their nests the fertilized eggs were kept in an incubator.
3. The first fertilized egg was turned every day to distribute the fluids evenly and then during the final seventy-two hours it was checked every hour.
4. Finally hisses grunts and cheeps were heard and the scientists tapped the egg to stimulate the chick to peck through the shell.
5. At last in April 1988 the chick did peck its way through the shell.
6. With the help of a puppeteer's glove designed to look like the head of an adult condor the chick was fed.
7. It grew eventually to a full-sized condor weighing twenty pounds and later eleven more chicks were hatched.
8. By 1990 the total number of condors reached forty for the first time in about twenty years and more chicks are expected.
9. "Reproducing condors in captivity is the key to their survival and now we know it can be done," said the park biologist.
10. Before long the scientists hope to begin releasing condors into the wild and people will again thrill to the sight of the great birds soaring over the land.

Source: *Discover,* July 1990

JOURNAL WRITING

Write the first three comma rules with a sentence to illustrate each.

COMMAS (RULES 4, 5, AND 6)

4. Put commas around the name of a person spoken to.

> I hope, Michelle, that you're going with me.
> David, you're an hour late.

5. Put commas around an expression that interrupts the flow of the sentence (such as *however, moreover, finally, therefore, of course, by the way, on the other hand, I am sure, I think*).

> I hope, of course, that they'll come.
> We took our plates, therefore, and got in line.
> It should, I think, take only an hour.

Read the preceding sentences aloud, and you'll hear how those expressions interrupt the flow of the sentence. Sometimes, however, such expressions flow smoothly into the sentence and don't need commas around them. Whether a word is an interrupter or not often depends on where it is in the sentence. If it's in the middle of a sentence, it's more likely to be an interrupter than if it's at the beginning or the end. The expressions that were interrupters in the preceding sentences are not interrupters in the following sentences and therefore don't require commas.

> Of course I hope they'll come.
> Therefore we took our plates and got in line.
> I think it should take only an hour.

Remember that when one of the above words like *however* comes between two independent clauses, that word always has a semicolon before it. It may also have a comma after it, especially if there seems to be a pause between the word and the rest of the sentence. (See p. 69)

> The taxi was late; *however,* I still made the plane.
> I didn't want to go; *furthermore,* I had no money.
> I wanted a good grade; *therefore* I worked harder.
> I spent hours on that course; *finally* I made an A.

Thus a word like *however* or *therefore* may be used in three ways:

> 1. as an interrupter (commas around it)
> 2. as a word that flows into the sentence (no commas needed)

3. as a connecting word between two independent clauses (semi-colon before it and often a comma after it)

6. Put commas around nonessential material.

Such material may be interesting, but the main idea of the sentence would be clear without it. In the following sentence

> Miriam Tilden, who heads the hospital volunteers, will speak tonight.

the clause *who leads the hospital volunteers* is not essential to the main idea of the sentence. Without it we still know exactly who the sentence is about and what she is going to do: Miriam Tilden will speak tonight. Therefore the nonessential material is set off from the rest of the sentence by commas to show that it could be left out. But in the following sentence

> The woman who heads the hospital volunteers will speak tonight.

the clause *who heads the hospital volunteers* is essential to the main idea of the sentence. Without it the sentence would read: The woman will speak tonight. We would have no idea which woman. The clause *who heads the hospital volunteers* is essential because it tells us which woman. It couldn't be left out. Therefore commas are not used around it. In this sentence

> *The Grapes of Wrath,* a novel by John Steinbeck, was a best-seller.

the words *a novel by John Steinbeck* could be left out, and we would still know the main meaning of the sentence: *The Grapes of Wrath* was a best-seller. Therefore the nonessential material is set off by commas to show that it could be left out. But in this sentence

> John Steinbeck's novel *The Grapes of Wrath* was a best-seller.

the title of the novel is essential. Without it, the sentence would read: John Steinbeck's novel was a best-seller. We would have no idea which of John Steinbeck's novels was a best-seller. Therefore the title couldn't be left out, and commas are not used around it.

The trick in deciding whether material is essential is to say, "Interesting, but is it necessary?"

EXERCISES

Punctuate these sentences according to Comma Rules 4, 5, and 6.

☐EXERCISE 1

1. This is the suit that I bought before Easter.
2. This suit which I bought before Easter is really too small.
3. The town where my parents grew up is a special place to me.
4. Atchison where my parents grew up is a special place to me.
5. She repainted the chair that had once belonged to her grandmother.
6. She repainted her grandmother's chair which had been in the attic.
7. Kilauea which was active when we were in Hawaii is one of the world's largest volcanoes.
8. We were lucky to see a volcano that was active while we were in Hawaii.
9. Queen City where we lived ten years ago has doubled in population.
10. The town where we lived ten years ago has doubled in population.

☐EXERCISE 2

1. The house that my grandfather built is still standing.
2. This house which my grandfather built now belongs to me.
3. My wife who teaches kindergarten doesn't get home until four.
4. Sybil who teaches kindergarten doesn't get home until four.
5. The senator who spoke to our group last night favors welfare reform.
6. Senator Sims who spoke to our group last night favors welfare reform.
7. Our Camaro which we bought a year ago was a good investment.
8. The car that we bought a year ago was a good investment.
9. Even a person who doesn't care for football would have enjoyed that game.
10. My dad who has never cared for football really enjoyed that game.

☐EXERCISE 3

1. Jason who had almost fallen asleep jumped when the instructor called on him.
2. He was of course flustered as he began to read his paper.
3. The class liked his paper however and told him why.
4. Most of the papers that were read today had been revised.
5. My paper I know was greatly improved by my revision.
6. Don't you think Connie that it's better than my previous draft?
7. Focused free writing which I've been trying lately has helped me.
8. But it's rewriting of course that really improves a paper.
9. Most of the papers that were read in class today will now be revised.
10. Rewrite our instructor says and then rewrite again.

☐EXERCISE 4

1. Most people I find don't know much about Duluth except that it's in Minnesota.
2. Last fall I spent two weeks which was my entire vacation in and around Duluth.
3. The fall colors which I observed on the twenty-seven-mile drive around the city were spectacular.
4. The aspens, maples, birches, and sumacs provide a panorama of red, gold, orange, and yellow that can't I think be surpassed anywhere.
5. The location of the city which is perched on an 800-foot ridge overlooking the blue water of Lake Superior is also spectacular.
6. Lake Superior which is 350 miles long, 160 miles wide, and in some places a quarter of a mile deep is the largest body of fresh water in the world.
7. One of Duluth's greatest attractions is the Aerial Lift Bridge which was built in 1929.
8. Instead of opening up as drawbridges do, it raises its entire center span which weighs nine hundred tons to let freighters pass under it.
9. I was especially interested in The Depot which was once a passenger station and where now a collection of trains rests on the original tracks of the 1892 depot.
10. The Depot also includes a large complex of museums which range from an art museum to a museum containing the model of an early logging camp.

☐EXERCISE 5

1. Last summer Jorge who's my best friend suggested that we take a backpacking trip.
2. We spent days of course trying to decide where to go.
3. After reading lots of travel magazines, we decided on Glacier National Park which has several ten-thousand-foot peaks and nearly fifty glaciers.
4. We had read that the park is composed of a million acres and furthermore that there are more than a thousand miles of hiking trails.
5. We decided therefore that there would be plenty to keep us busy.
6. We took a bus to the park entrance and then spent the first evening listening to a park naturalist talk about glaciers which we knew nothing about.
7. We decided immediately that our first hike would be to Grinnell Glacier which is one of the two largest glaciers in the park.
8. It was a twelve-mile, all-day hike, but it was beyond a doubt the highlight of our whole trip.

9. A park naturalist who happened to be taking a group along the glacier explained that most glaciers move from six to thirty feet a year.
10. Their movement he explained depends on four things: their size, the slope of the land, the temperature, and the amount of water in the ice.

□EXERCISE 6

1. Ski resorts in the East which used to worry about the weather now give the weather little thought.
2. New snowmaking systems which are more efficient than the old ones provide twelve different kinds of snow, such as base, corn, frozen, granular, and machine.
3. The only kind of snow they don't provide obviously is real snow.
4. The new systems make more snow for every gallon of water and every cubic foot of air pumped, and they are able furthermore to make snow in warmer and more humid weather.
5. Killington resort in Vermont which has ninety trails and sixteen lifts can now operate from mid-October to late May or even mid-June.
6. Stowe in Vermont which advertises that it has more than twenty feet of natural snowfall per year supplements the natural snow with one of New England's most extensive snowmaking systems.
7. The snowmaking systems however are expensive.
8. Costs at Hunter Mountain in New York for one season were estimated at $1 million.
9. It's not surprising therefore that the price of ski-lift tickets has increased.
10. The extra money beyond a doubt goes to the making of snow.

□EXERCISE 7

1. Jeannette Rankin who had a campaign fund of less than $700 was in 1916 the first woman ever elected to Congress.
2. Rankin a Republican from Montana always voted according to her convictions.
3. In 1917 therefore she voted against war with Germany.
4. She was jeered as a traitor and told furthermore that she would harm the woman suffrage movement if she took such a stand.
5. She voted nevertheless against the war because she had a lifetime conviction against war.
6. War she said had always seemed to her the worst way ever devised for settling disputes.
7. After Pearl Harbor which caused a great wave of public sentiment for war she cast her vote of *no* in Congress against the 388 who voted *aye* for the war with Japan.

8. William Allen White editor of the *Emporia Gazette* wrote, "The *Gazette* entirely disagrees with the wisdom of her position. But, Lord, it was a brave thing to do."
9. And John F. Kennedy writing some 17 years later praised the courage of the congresswoman from Montana.
10. Her vote against the war with Japan ended her political career, but years later at the age of 87 she led 5,000 women to the foot of Capitol Hill to protest the hostilities in Vietnam.

Can you insert the nine necessary commas in this student paper? No answers are provided.

☐**EXERCISE 8**

MISSING ME?

During the summer I would ask my dad if he'd miss me when I went away to college and he would say, "Are you kidding? For once the phone will remain on the hook, the upstairs bedroom will be clean, and the house will be peaceful." I would laugh, not being sure whether he meant it or not. I thought he didn't because I was very close to my dad. Yet there was always that feeling that maybe he wasn't joking. I admitted everything he said was true. I did talk on the phone a lot and even received calls at two in the morning. Sure my bedroom was messy. I never seemed to have time to clean it. I wasn't at home enough to make the house noisy but when I was I guess I did play my stereo loud and I did yell and talk a lot.

My dad is the type to kid around though. If I was ever in a bad mood he was there to cheer me up. If I ever had a problem he was there to help. Maybe I *was* a problem for him though. Maybe this time he wasn't joking.

As I drove slowly toward college that afternoon I found myself feeling more and more upset and as the days went by I became more disturbed. I hated to see our good relationship fading.

Then one day after I had been at college a couple of weeks I got a letter from my dad. . . . It began, "Gad, how I miss you honey."

JOURNAL WRITING

Write six sentences using the six comma rules given in the following box.

Review of the Comma

THE SIX COMMA RULES

1. Put a comma before *and, but, for, or, nor, yet, so* when they connect two independent clauses.
2. Put a comma between three or more items in a series.
3. Put a comma after an introductory expression or before an after-thought.
4. Put commas around the name of a person spoken to.
5. Put commas around an interrupter, like *however* or *moreover.*
6. Put commas around nonessential material.

Add the necessary commas to these sentences.

1. Many Americans do not know about Highway 1 which goes over the ocean.
2. It is 109 miles long and with its forty-two bridges links the string of keys or islands that run from Miami to Key West.
3. The keys which go southwestward from the mainland of Florida form a dividing line between the Gulf of Mexico and the Atlantic Ocean.
4. The keys are great places for shell collecting bird-watching and fishing.
5. Shell collectors who say the keys beaches are the best places in the United States for shells have the best luck just after high tide.
6. Bird-watchers are interested in the herons pelicans and egrets that stop at the keys on their migratory routes.
7. Unknown to many people there lies just offshore the only living coral reef in the continental United States.
8. Many kinds of coral abound but the sharp edges of many corals must be handled with gloves.
9. Many Spanish galleons were shipwrecked on the razor-sharp reefs of the keys and sank with their treasures.
10. On Grassy Key is the Dolphin Research Center which trains dolphins for show business or for experiments.
11. Of the six endangered species found in the keys the most interesting is the Key Deer which stands only three feet tall.

12. Unfortunately the Key Deer cross the traveled highways and about sixty are killed each year which is more than are born in a year.
13. Among the famous artists and writers who have found inspiration at Key West over the years are James Audubon Hart Crane and Ernest Hemingway.

QUOTATION MARKS .

Put quotation marks around the exact words of a speaker (direct quotation), but not around an indirect quotation.

> He said, "I'll go." (his exact words)
> She said she would do it. (not her exact words)
> He said that he would go. (not his exact words)

Whenever *that* precedes the words of a speaker (as in the last example), it indicates that the words are not a direct quotation and should not have quotation marks around them.

If the speaker says more than one sentence, quotation marks are used only before and after the entire speech.

> He said, "I'll go. It's no trouble. I'll be there at six."

The words telling who is speaking are set off with a comma unless, of course, a question mark or exclamation mark is needed.

> "I'll go," he said.
> "Do you want me to go?" he asked.

Every quotation begins with a capital letter. But when a quotation is broken, the second part doesn't begin with a capital letter unless it's a new sentence.

> "Ninety percent of the friction of daily life," said Arnold Bennett, "is caused by tone of voice."
> "A friend is a person with whom I may be sincere," said Emerson. "Before him, I may think aloud."

Begin a new paragraph with each change of speaker.

> "Will you come with me?" I asked Barbara as I got up and walked toward the door.
> "What for?" she said.
> "Just because I want you to," I replied.

Put quotation marks around the name of a short story, poem, song, essay, TV program episode, radio program, or other short work. For a longer work such as a book, newspaper, magazine, play, record album or CD, movie, or title of a TV series, use underlining (which means it would be italicized in print).

> I like Robert Frost's short poem "Dust of Snow."
> James Thurber's short story "The Secret Life of Walter Mitty" is found in his book *My World—and Welcome to It.*
> I read about it in *Newsweek.*
> Did you see the episode of *ER* titled "Dead of Winter?"
> My parents listen to National Public Radio's *All Things Considered* every day.

Indent and single space, without quotation marks, all quotations of more than five lines.

The psychiatrist Karl Menninger believes that generosity is a good indicator of a person's mental health. He says:

> Generous people are rarely mentally ill people. On the other hand, let's not get critical of some of our stingy friends. Remember that stinginess is an illness. Some don't dare give even if they have much money. They might run out. My dear friends, of course you are going to run out. You can't take it with you. I don't know how many hundreds of my patients are now asleep in the graveyard, leaving behind them far more money . . . than their children can amicably divide. . . .

Menninger goes on to say that the more generous people are, the more mentally healthy—but that generosity includes more than just giving money.

EXERCISES

Punctuate the quotations, and underline or put quotation marks around each title.

☐EXERCISE 1

1. Let's get something to eat she said.

2. Do you want to go now or after the movie he asked.

3. Why not both times she said.

4. Snow and adolescence are the only problems that disappear if you ignore them long enough my father says.

5. Some people can stay longer in an hour than others can in a week said William Dean Howells.

6. After her weekend visitors left, she remarked that guests always bring pleasure—if not in the coming, then in the going.

7. If people could be got into the woods, even for once, John Muir said, to hear the trees speak for themselves, all difficulties in the way of forest preservation would vanish.

8. With all its sham, drudgery, and broken dreams said Adlai Stevenson it is still a beautiful world.

9. We went to see The Wild Duck, a play by Henrik Ibsen.

10. Our future as a nation is going to depend not so much on what happens in outer space as on what happens in inner space—the space between our ears said the lecturer.

☐EXERCISE 2

1. The actions of some children said Will Rogers suggest that their parents embarked on the sea of matrimony without a paddle.

2. The best time to tackle a small problem said my father is before he grows up.

3. When Mom goes shopping says Kip she leaves no store unturned.

4. I agree with the Spanish proverb how beautiful it is to do nothing and then rest afterward.

5. He found her munching chocolates and reading a book entitled Eat, Drink, and Be Buried.

6. Mark Twain said when I was a boy of fourteen, my father was so ignorant I could hardly stand to have the old man around. But when I got to be twenty-one, I was astonished at how much the old man had learned in seven years.

7. Mark Twain said the parts of the Bible which give me the most trouble are those I understand the best.

8. Work consists of whatever a body is obliged to do, and play consists of whatever a body is not obliged to do said Mark Twain.

9. On observing the great number of civic statues, Cato, a famous Roman, remarked I would rather people would ask why there is not a statue of Cato than why there is.

10. One does not complain about water because it is wet said Abraham Maslow nor about rocks because they are hard.

☐EXERCISE 3

1. I've just read Barn Burning, a short story by William Faulkner.

2. The construction of an airplane wrote Charles Lindbergh is simple compared to the evolutionary achievement of a bird.

3. If I had the choice Lindbergh continued I would rather have birds than airplanes.

4. Of war, George Bernard Shaw said that the men should all shoot their officers and go home.

5. An art critic once said that there are three kinds of people in the world: those who can't stand Picasso, those who can't stand Raphael, and those who've never heard of either of them.

6. Pablo Casals, the great cellist, spent hours on a single phrase. He said people say I play as easily as a bird sings. If they only knew how much effort their bird has put into his song.

7. As it is the mark of great minds to say many things in a few words wrote La Rochefoucauld so it is the mark of little minds to use many words to say nothing.

8. William James said that the essence of genius is to know what to overlook.

9. Whatever you have you must either use or lose said Henry Ford.

10. A span of time either leaves you better off or worse off wrote John Gardner there is no neutral time.

□EXERCISE 4

1. Finish every day and be done with it said Ralph Waldo Emerson tomorrow is a new day.

2. Life can only be understood backward said Kierkegaard but it must be lived forward.

3. The most valuable of all talents is that of never using two words when one will do said Thomas Jefferson.

4. The only conquests that are permanent and leave no regrets Napoleon said are our conquests over ourselves.

5. Nearly all men can stand adversity, but if you want to test a man's character, give him power said Lincoln.

6. Freud said that to have mental health a person has to be able to love and to work.

7. In the novel Fathers and Sons by Turgenev the main character says that the chief thing is to be able to devote oneself.

8. Nobody can carry three watermelons under one arm says a Spanish proverb.

9. The taller the bamboo grows the lower it bends says a Japanese proverb.

10. The man who does not do more work than he's paid for said Abraham Lincoln isn't worth what he gets.

□EXERCISE 5

1. The cost of a thing is the amount of what I call life which is required to be exchanged for it, immediately or in the long run said Thoreau.

2. A man is rich said Thoreau in proportion to the number of things he can afford to let alone.

3. Viewing the multitude of articles exposed for sale in the marketplace, Socrates remarked how many things there are that I do not want.

4. What! Sell land? said Tecumseh, a Shawnee Indian chief. As well sell air and water. The Great Spirit gave them in common to all—the air to breathe, the water to drink, and the land to live upon.

5. Perhaps the most valuable result of all education said Thomas Huxley is the ability to make yourself do the thing you have to do, when it ought to be done, whether you like it or not.

6. James B. Conant, former president of Harvard, said that a liberal education is what remains after all you have learned has been forgotten.

7. Education does not mean teaching people to know what they do not know said John Ruskin it means teaching them to behave as they do not behave.

8. Sometimes when fate kicks us and we finally land and look around, we find we have been kicked upstairs said Carl Sandburg.

□EXERCISE 6

1. By the year 2000, if present trends continue, said the professor the world will be losing one plant or animal species every hour of every day.

2. What's so important a student asked about the extinction of a pupfish or a coneflower?

3. It may be of immense importance! the professor continued half of our modern medicines, for example, can be traced to wild organisms.

4. And I suppose wild plants could give us more medicines another student volunteered.

5. Right said the professor the source for our next miracle drug could be one of the plants that are endangered right now.

6. What can we do about it another student wanted to know.

7. The professor said that we can contribute to funds for buying lands that are home to the endangered plants and animals.

CAPITAL LETTERS

Capitalize

1. The first word of every sentence.

2. The first word of every direct quotation.

He said, "We've jogged two miles."
"We've jogged two miles," he said, "and I feel great." (The *and* is not capitalized because it doesn't begin a new sentence.)
"We've jogged two miles," he said. "It made me feel great." (*It* is capitalized because it begins a new sentence.)

3. The first, last, and every important word in a title. Don't capitalize prepositions, short connecting words, the *to* in front of a verb, or *a, an, the.*

I've been reading Bulfinch's *The Age of Fable.*
We read Swift's "A Modest Proposal" last year.
The musical *Once Upon a Mattress* is based on the fairy tale "The Princess and the Pea."

4. Names of people, places, languages, races, and nationalities.

Grandfather Davis	Japan	Chicano
Uganda	English	Indian
Mother Teresa	New York City	Native American

5. Names of months, days of the week, and special days, but not the seasons.

February	Fourth of July	spring
Wednesday	Thanksgiving	summer
Election Day	Kwanza	

6. A title of relationship if it takes the place of the person's name. If *my* (or *your, her, his, our, their*) is in front of the word, a capital is not used.

I think Mother wrote to her.	*but*	I think my mother wrote to her.
She visited Aunt Rhonda.	*but*	She visited her aunt.
We spoke with Granddad.	*but*	We spoke with our granddad.

7. Names of particular people or things, but not general ones.

I spoke to Professor Brown.   *but*   I spoke to the professor.
We sailed on the Wabash River. *but*   We sailed on the river.
Are you from the Midwest?   *but*   We turned west.
I take Art 300 and French 101.   *but*   I take art and French.
I went to Dwight High School.   *but*   I was in high school last year.
He goes to Clark College.   *but*   He's going to college now.
We enjoyed the Guggenheim   *but*   We enjoyed the museum.
   Museum.

EXERCISES

Add the necessary capital letters.

☐EXERCISE 1

1. Classes started here at Ironwood junior college the day after labor day, and I'm now into my third week.
2. I'm taking history, english, accounting, and spanish.
3. I thought I wouldn't like english, but I do.
4. I think the professor is an interesting lecturer.
5. Yesterday she read Robert Frost's poem "The death of the hired man."
6. For tomorrow we're to read Eudora Welty's short story "A worn path."
7. In high school I seldom studied, but college has changed all that.
8. All my professors demand good english in written work.
9. Therefore I'm grateful for the good start I got in spelling and punctuation when I attended Sequoia high school.
10. Next semester I plan to take psychology 101, history 210, and English 120; then the following semester I'll take math, physics, and spanish.

☐EXERCISE 2

1. My parents and I took a long trip last summer.
2. We started on the fourth of July and didn't get back until the second of August.
3. First we drove east to Boston to visit my grandfather.
4. He was born in the east and has now gone back there to live.
5. Then we started to drive to Canada, but we came to a detour that took us first south, then west, and then finally north.
6. Eventually we got to Algonquin park and spent a few days there.
7. Then mom wanted to see a friend in Michigan, and dad wanted to stop at a little lake near lake Superior for fishing.

8. Our next stop was at the Indiana dunes state park southeast of Chicago, where we camped out on the sand under the stars.
9. There my mom tried to teach my dad and me some of the constellations.
10. We didn't learn many, however, beyond cassiopeia and orion.

□EXERCISE 3

1. My granddad used to take us boating on the river on weekends.
2. The Missouri river has some exceptionally swift currents.
3. However, granddad was always able to maneuver the boat safely.
4. When I went away to college, I of course had no time for boating.
5. Then in the summer I got a job as a counselor at a camp near Barren river lake, and again I had time for boating.
6. I'll always be grateful for the training granddad gave me.
7. Now my plan is to go far away to finish college.
8. I'd like to go to Weber state college in Ogden, Utah.
9. I've always wanted to go to a large state college, and I've always wanted to go to Utah.
10. Maybe I'll even be able to do some boating on one of the rivers out there.

□EXERCISE 4

1. I read an article in *newsweek* that amazed me.
2. The American lung association has a new supporter for their anti-smoking campaign.
3. It is Patrick Reynolds, a young actor and an heir to the fortunes of the J. R. Reynolds tobacco company.
4. That company is the second largest cigarette maker in the united states.
5. Patrick Reynolds' grandfather helped develop the company and left a fortune to his heirs.
6. Patrick quit smoking in 1984 and sold all his shares in the company.
7. His father had died of emphysema at 58, and Patrick says his anti-smoking views are rooted in personal concern.
8. Now he appears on the antismoking ads of the American lung association.
9. Some people have asked, "aren't you biting the hand that feeds you?"
10. He has answered, "it's the same hand that has killed millions and may kill millions more."

□EXERCISE 5

1. While we spent the winter in Florida a couple of years ago, everyone in the family went to college.

2. My dad decided he needed to know more about computers.
3. So he enrolled in an evening course in computer science at St. Petersburg junior college.
4. My mom hopes eventually to get a B.A. and so took a correspondence course in medieval literature.
5. I took a course in computer science at the university of Tampa.
6. My sister went to a denominational college near where we were staying.
7. It's a small college, and we wondered why she chose it.
8. "I'd rather be a big duck in a little pond," she said, "than a little duck in a big pond."
9. She had nothing but praise for her instructors and the courses.
10. When we were at home, all we talked about was who was going to the best college.

☐EXERCISE 6

1. Next summer I plan to drive to the yukon.
2. On my way back I'll stop in some of the Canadian provinces.
3. I've never been to Prince Albert park in northern Saskatchewan.
4. I'd also like to see lake of the woods in Manitoba with its hundreds of lakes.
5. My uncle used to tell us children about them.
6. He would come to our house on summer evenings and tell us stories.
7. Usually aunt Agatha came with him.
8. My aunt and uncle had no children and practically adopted my brother and me.
9. I have been to Ontario, but I'd like to see more of Toronto.
10. Maybe I might even get as far as some of the eastern provinces.

☐EXERCISE 7

1. I have been reading some magazines that are new to me.
2. I used to read time and newsweek, but this week I am reading the smithsonian.
3. In it I found an interesting article entitled "life for lefties."
4. I had always thought that people were left-handed just because they didn't bother to use the correct hand.
5. That article told he how wrong I had been.
6. Ten to fifteen percent of people are left-handed, and they are that way from birth.
7. It's not that they are just carelessly using the wrong hand.
8. Some of the greatest artists have been left-handed: Raphael, Leonardo, Holbein, and Picasso.

9. Some lefties include presidents George Bush, Gerald Ford, Harry Truman, and Bill Clinton.
10. So I have now learned that people who use the left hand are not just being careless.

☐EXERCISE 8

1. Our family drove through the midwest and the west this spring.
2. Mother and dad had never had a real vacation before.
3. I had never gone sailing on a river until I sailed on the Red river.
4. We visited the Badlands of South Dakota, but we missed seeing mount Rushmore.
5. My mother particularly enjoyed seeing Yellowstone national park.
6. I'm impressed with all the national parks in our country.
7. My dad liked the drive through the groves of redwood trees in California.
8. Both mother and dad enjoyed walking along the Pacific ocean.
9. Then we left Marin county and drove across the golden gate bridge.
10. I like the climate of the west coast, but my summer job is in the east.

☐EXERCISE 9

1. All of us children except my brother Ned will be in college this fall.
2. Ned graduated last spring from Pasadena city college in California.
3. Last summer he worked for the Ford motor company but was not there long enough to receive any company benefits.
4. Now he works for a refinery of the Mobil oil company, which is 10 miles from our house.
5. "I need a motorcycle," he said, "and I'm going to buy one."
6. He asked dad for advice about buying a motorcycle.
7. "You know more about them," dad said, "than I do."
8. Ned then went to the public library and found an article entitled "How to buy your first motorcycle."
9. He looked at motorcycles all summer.
10. Then he finally bought one and now rides to work each day.

Review of Punctuation and Capital Letters

Punctuate these sentences. They include all the rules for punctuation and capitalization you have learned. Compare your answers carefully with those at the back of the book. Most sentences have several errors.

☐EXERCISE 1

1. The Taj Mahal which is in Agra is often called the most beautiful building in the world.

2. Do you read Time or Newsweek.

3. I'm glad it's snowing now we can go skiing tomorrow.

4. Skiing skating and tobogganing are our chief winter sports.

5. Figure skating which I'm just learning takes hours of practice.

6. His knapsack contained the following items food matches and a canteen.

7. The sign in the dentist's office read support your dentist eat candy.

8. Sydney J. Harris says it seems to me that growing older imposes a duty upon us to get more like a peach on the inside as we get more like a prune on the outside.

9. A little old lady from Boston refused to travel saying Why should I travel I'm already here.

10. You can get the document by writing to the Superintendent of Documents Government Printing Office Washington DC.

11. My mother who is not a writer herself is still a good critic of my writing.

12. He tried to improve his vocabulary by looking up new words by keeping word lists and by using the words in conversation.

13. Children have never been good at listening to their elders says James Baldwin but they have never failed to imitate them.

14. Reading improves your understanding of human nature writing improves your understanding of yourself.

15. One tree can make three million matches one match can burn three million trees.

16. An arabian proverb says I had no shoes and complained until I met a man who had no feet.

Next you will find some quotations from famous people. Does one of them apply to you? Or could you profit from following one of them? Choose one that interests you and write your reaction to it. This is the first time you have been asked to write this kind of paper. Simply write as if you are talking to a friend.

Quotations by Famous People

The best way out is always through.

Robert Frost

When you get to the end of your rope, tie a knot and hang on.

Franklin D. Roosevelt

Great Spirit, help me never to judge another until I have walked in his moccasins for two weeks.

Sioux Indian Prayer

Mend your speech a little,
Lest it mar your fortunes.

Shakespeare

We can easily forgive a child who is afraid of the dark; the real tragedy of life is when men are afraid of the light.

Plato

Don't be afraid to take a big step if one is indicated. You can't cross a chasm in two small jumps.

David Lloyd George

A friend is a person with whom I may be sincere. Before him I may think aloud.

Emerson

Dost thou love life? Then do not squander time, for that is the stuff life is made up of.

Benjamin Franklin

Faults are thick where love is thin.

Danish proverb

There is nothing noble in being superior to some other man. The true nobility is in being superior to your former self.

Hindu proverb

Poetry is a synthesis of hyacinths and biscuits.

Carl Sandburg

Sometimes when fate kicks us and we finally land and look around, we find that we have been kicked upstairs.

Carl Sandburg

With all its sham, drudgery, and broken dreams, it is still a beautiful world.

Adlai Stevenson

Education does not mean teaching people to know what they do not know; it means teaching them to behave as they do not behave.

John Ruskin

The great pianist Paderewski summed up a life of unremitting effort in this remark: "Before I was a master, I was a slave."

Proofreading Exercise 1

Try to find the nine errors in this student paper. You may have to read the paper several times to find them all. Challenge your instructor to find all nine on the first try!

THOSE FAULTY PARTS

I was only ten years old, but I had all the confidence of a great scientist. I had already built a little electric motor and fixed the electric parts in all the toys anyone would bring me. And now I had a magazine article that told how to build a simple battery-powered radio. The directions looked straight-forward all I needed was the parts.

My world extended only as far as my bicycle could take me, so the only place I knew that sold radio parts was the TV repair shop five blocks away. I don't no what the men their first thought of a ten-year-old kid trying to build a radio but I persisted until one of them gathered up the parts and sold them to me. They cost a few weeks' allowance money, but I new it was going to be worth it.

Well, after a few days of work, I had it finish. Admittedly, my wiring didnt look as neat as that in the picture. As a matter of fact, those people had used a few more wires than I had, but I didn't feel that all of them were really necessary.

But my radio didn't work! And my ten-year-old mind concluded that it must be that the TV repair shop had sold me faulty parts. I bicycled back with my new radio under my arm and demanded an explanation I was upset. After a long discussion, one of the men finally took my radio and started working on it. I think he was afraid I might cry or something.

In about half an hour, and after many changes, he got it working.

"No charge kid," he said.

"Thank you," I said in my most polite voice, thrilled at the sound of music coming from my radio.

What a feeling of accomplishment! It was as if Id invented something great. I guess the TV repairman must have had a bit of feeling of accomplishment too as a beaming ten-year-old rode away with a little radio that worked under his arm.

Proofreading Exercise 2

This student paper is marred by one fragment and three run-together sentences. Make the necessary corrections.

I DON'T WANT TO

I must have tried to give up smoking a dozen times. Sometimes I'd last a month. And sometimes only a day or two. Always I'd start again. Then it hit me. The trouble was I didn't really want to stop I was one of those who say they want to stop but really don't. If people truly wanted to stop, I reasoned, they would. What I really needed, then, was simply to not want to smoke.

One day I added up all the negative aspects of smoking—the cost, the yellow stains on my fingers, the nervousness, the bad breathe, the rotten taste in my mouth every morning, the smoker's cough, the danger to my health. Then, too, I told myself that smoking was a sign of weakness. I was unable to control myself I was caught in a habit that big tobacco companies were continuously promoting. That bothered me. I was, against my will, doing exactly what some big companies wanted me to do it was then I decided that I really didn't want to smoke.

The day I decided I didn't want to smoke, I simply stopped. Oh, it took a couple of weeks of effort to break the habit, but it's been three years now, and I haven't had another cigarette. All it took was just not to want to.

Proofreading Exercise 3

Here is another student paper to proofread. This one has seven errors.

CURB THAT ENTHUSIASM

There we were, the two of us, in an eight-foot rubber raft, approaching Three Forks Rapids. Neither of us had ever tried river rafting before and it was scary. We had our life jackets strapped on tight and were bracing ourselves for what might come.

As we were swept along in the incredibly swift current, I held the two oars and tried to direct the raft. Nick, in the front, was suppose to watch for rocks and yell out which direction to head but already the thunder of the water hurtling through the rapids had drowned out his voice. Anyway I was really rowing as hard as I could just to keep the raft pointing downstream, let alone directing it more specifically.

Then came the first big drop! Its an amazing feeling riding over a sudden four-foot drop in a river. But somehow we stayed upright and landed below in the white foaming water. We cheered and congratulated each other for a moment but then braced ourselves for the next big drop coming right up.

Amazingly we did it. We managed to keep the raft afloat again with both of us still in it.

"Great!" I yelled. "We made 'em both."

"We're good!" Nick shouted.

Giving a whoop, he turned around but then as we yelled and laughed, we both happen to lean the same way, and sure enough, after running the rapids unscathed, we now found the raft tiping sideways, and over we went into the calm water. . . .

The *next* time, we told each other as we righted the raft and climbed back on board, we're going to curb our enthusiasm.

Comprehensive Test

In these sentences you'll find all the errors that have been discussed in the entire text. Correct them by adding apostrophes, punctuation, and capital letters and by crossing out incorrect expressions and writing the corrections above them. Most sentences have several errors. A perfect—or almost perfect—score will mean you've mastered the first part of the text.

1. Its useless to wait hes probably not coming.

2. If one wants a larger vocabulary you should study word roots.

3. Spending entirely too much time on that one coarse last semester.

4. Dad ask my sister and me to water the lawn we was glad to do it.

5. While they were waiting for there daughter, they're engine stalled.

6. I cant decide whether to finish my math, study my history, or whether I should take it easy for a change.

7. If you're going to be hear Dawn you can answer the phone for me.

8. Your going with me, aren't you.

9. We freshmen helped a upperclass student with registration he really appreciated it.

10. I was quiet sure that Rons car was in the driveway.

11. When we were on our trip we visited some cities in the south.

12. Which had many beautiful old homes and lovely gardens.

13. Its Mr. Petersons car but hes not driving it.

14. Each of the students are planning a individual report.

15. Looking under the car, the missing baseball was found.

16. Christines grades are always higher than Elizabeths.

17. Ill be ready in a minute Jeanne said.

18. This semester I'm taking french, history, and english.

19. The united nations receives more brickbats than bravos yet it remains the only real hope for peace.

20. She told her sister she needed a new purse.

21. They didnt think however that they would have time to come back.

22. She was suppose to read the short story The Elephant's Child from Rudyard Kipling's book Just So Stories.

23. Whether you agree with me or whether you follow your own ideas.

24. We waited as long as we could than we went on without her.

25. Whats done to children, they will do to society wrote Karl Menninger.

Writing

4

4 | Writing

You learn to write by *writing*—not by reading long discussions *about* writing. Therefore the instructions in this section are brief. In fact, they are boiled down to just eight steps that you need to take to write good papers. Take these eight steps, one at a time, and you'll write more effectively and also more easily. Here are the steps:

EIGHT STEPS TO BETTER WRITING

      I. Do some free writing.
     II. Limit your topic.
   III. Write a thesis statement.
   IV. Support your thesis with reasons or points.
    V. Organize your paper from your thesis.
   VI. Organize each paragraph.
  VII. Write and rewrite.
 VIII. Proofread ALOUD.

I. DO SOME FREE WRITING

"Writing is good for us," Oliver Wendell Holmes said, "because it brings our thoughts out into the open, as a boy turns his pockets inside out to see what is in them." Try "turning your pockets inside out" by writing as fast as you can for five minutes. Write anything that comes into your mind. Put your thoughts down as fast as they come. What you write may not make sense, but that doesn't matter. Write fast. Don't stop a moment. Don't even take your pen off the page. If you can't think of anything to write, just write, "I can't think of anything to write," over and over until something occurs to you. Look at your watch and begin.

This free writing should limber up your mind and your pen so that you'll write more freely.

Now try another kind of free writing—focused free writing. Write for five minutes as fast as you can, but this time stick to one subject—travel.

Look at your watch and begin.

Did you focus on travel that long? Did you think of family trips, of backpacking, of the most beautiful place you've ever seen, of trips to your grandmother's when you were small, of places you'd like to see?

You didn't have time to include all those things of course. Now write for ten minutes and add more to your discussion of travel. Begin.

Focused free writing is a good way to begin any writing. When you are assigned a paper, try writing for ten minutes putting down all your thoughts on the subject. It will let you see what material you have and will help you figure out what aspect of the subject (what topic) to write about.

II. LIMIT YOUR TOPIC

Finding the right topic is sometimes the hardest part of writing. For one thing, you need to limit your topic so that you can handle it in a paper of three hundred to five hundred words. The subject of travel, which you used for free writing, was obviously too big. You could limit it by saying

A canoe trip
Our best family vacation
Backpacking

but even those topics are too big. Keep making your topic smaller

Backpacking in the wilderness

and smaller

Backpacking in Algonquin Park

and smaller

One day of backpacking in Algonquin Park

Now you have a topic limited enough to write about in a short paper.

Usually the more you limit your topic, the better your paper will be, for then you'll have room to add plenty of specific details. And it's specific details that will interest your reader.

The following two assignments emphasize the first two Steps to Better Writing—doing some free writing and limiting your topic.

In these two assignments we are not going to worry about paragraph structure and many of the things we'll consider later. Just present your ideas the way you would if you were talking to someone. Our only goal in these two assignments is to write something others will find interesting.

Assignment 1   A Significant Incident

Think of some incident in your life that had a profound effect upon you. It might be from your childhood or from later years, but it should be an incident that had so much significance for you that you will long remember it.

First do some free writing telling about the experience. Put down all the details you can think of. For example, if you're going to tell about the time you won a trophy, you'll want to say more than that it was a great moment. You'll want to tell what you saw at that moment, what you heard, how you felt. If you are groping for details, remember your five senses— sight, hearing, smell, taste, and touch. Each of them may call forth some details you hadn't thought of before. It's specific details that will help your reader live the experience with you.

When you've done all the free writing you can, then make sure your topic is limited. If you're writing about winning a trophy, you won't tell about the entire season but only about actually receiving the award.

Before you start to write, you might like to read a student paper on this assignment. This student at first was having so many difficulties with spelling and sentence structure that his paper was almost impossible to read, but after a number of rewritings, it is now clear and understandable. He had something interesting to say, and it was worth his while to get rid of the errors so that his paper can be read easily.

JASON

Two years ago at the district wrestling tournament, where I was wrestling with the team, halfway through the meet I noticed an apparently retarded boy talking to and annoying everyone. Some of the crowd moved to other seats. Everybody was watching and laughing, including the guys on the bench where my team was seated. I leaned over to the guy next to me, whom I've known for several years, and I said, "Ron, look at that weirdo up there." Ron then replied proudly, "He's my older brother Jason. He's a mongoloid." I felt like a real jackass!

Later when there was a break in the tournament, Ron's brother came down on the mat and attempted to wrestle like Ron does. Of course everyone was watching Jason in hysterical laughter. Ron then lovingly and proudly walked onto the mat and embraced Jason, and they walked off together. The whole gymnasium hushed, and a tear came into my eye.

Now write your paper for this assignment. Imagine you're telling someone about your significant experience, and write what you would say. Remember that fully as important as making your paper mechanically correct is making it so interesting that your readers will enjoy it.

Finally, spend some time thinking of a good title. Just as you're more likely to read a magazine article with a catchy title, so your readers will be more eager to read your paper if you give it a good title. (And remember that every important word in a title is capitalized.) Which of these titles from student papers would make you want to read further?

An Interesting Experience	Inchworms Get There
Knees Shaking	My Favorite Class
Toss It Away	Say Cheese
Jail Outside a Jail	

Your paper should be typed or prepared on a word processor, double-spaced, or written legibly in ink on 8½-by-11-inch paper on one side only. A 1½-inch margin should be left on each side of the page for your instructor's comments. The beginning of each paragraph should be indented about five spaces.

Part of the success of your paper depends on how it looks. The same paper typed sloppily or neatly might well receive different grades. If, however, when you do your final proofreading, you find a word misspelled or a word left out, make neat corrections in pen.

Assignment 2   A Place I'll Never Forget

What place means more to you than any other place in the world? It might be a place you know now or one you knew in childhood—a playroom, your workshop, a backyard, a playing field . . .

Do some free writing to bring to your mind specific details that will help your reader see your place. Telling some events that happened there will also help your reader participate in your memory of it.

Here's a student paper, a third draft. With each draft the writer added specific details about what he saw, what he did, and how he felt. Now you can visualize the place and understand how the writer feels about it.

THE SCHOOLYARD

It's the schoolyard that I remember. Oh sure, things went on inside the school—lessons, reports, projects—but it's the schoolyard that I'll never forget.

All the other paperboys and I would hang around the schoolyard after finishing our paper routes. We'd have toy car races in the dirt or play with waterguns or trade baseball cards. The older boys wouldn't let us play baseball with them, and of course the girls were sissies who none of us liked, but we never tired of our own entertainment.

We even had our own version of baseball. We'd make a big square "Strike Zone" on the school wall with chalk, and then a batter would stand in front of it and try to hit the baseball (actually a tennis ball) that someone would pitch. When the batter had three strikes, a player from the other team would come up to bat. I've never played a baseball game since then that could come up to those games in excitement.

In the winter we'd throw snowballs at each other or at the girls—but never at the bigger boys. When it was really cold, we'd play hockey on the schoolyard rink. I remember putting on my skates in the warmth of our kitchen and then walking the two blocks to school with my skates on.

And there were big events too, like Athletics Day when the whole school turned out for races. Once our fifth grade lined up on one side of the schoolyard and then at the starting gun raced as fast as we could to the other side. That was a great day for me because at the finish a teacher grabbed me and took me over to the finalists' table, where I was given a little pin for second place. I still have the pin.

That schoolyard is a part of me.

Now write a description of your place that will help your reader picture it and feel its importance to you.

III. WRITE A THESIS STATEMENT

The most important thing to keep in mind, no matter what you are writing, is the idea you want to get across to your reader. No matter whether you are writing a paragraph or a longer piece, you must have in mind a single idea that you want to express. In a longer paper such an idea is called a thesis statement; in a paragraph it's called a topic sentence, but they mean the same thing—an idea you want to get across.

The limited topic on page 189, "One day of backpacking in Algonquin Park," doesn't make any point. What about that day? What did it do for you? What point about that day would you like to present to your reader? You might write.

> One day of backpacking in Algonquin Park taught me the importance of getting in shape beforehand.

or

> One day of backpacking in Algonquin Park showed me that I have more resourcefulness than I was aware of.

or

> One day of backpacking in Algonquin Park made me a confirmed back-packer.

Now you have said something specific. **When you write in one sentence the single limited point you want to present to your reader, you have written a thesis statement.**

All good writers have a thesis in mind when they begin to write. Whether they are writing articles, novels, short stories, poems, or plays, they have in mind an idea they want to present to the reader. They may develop it in various ways, but behind whatever they write is their ruling thought, their reason for writing, their thesis.

For any writing assignment, after you have done some free writing and limited your topic, your next step is to write a thesis statement. As you write your thesis statement, keep two things in mind:

1. **A thesis statement must be a sentence** (not merely a topic) **with a subject and a verb.**

TOPIC	THESIS
One day of backpacking in	One day of backpacking in Algon-
Algonquin Park	quin Park made me a con-
	firmed backpacker.

TOPIC	THESIS
Quitting smoking	My decision to quit smoking was the best decision I ever made.
Poachers in Yosemite	New laws are needed to protect Yosemite from poachers.

2. **A thesis statement must be a statement that you can explain or defend** (not simply a well-known fact).

FACT	THESIS
Many accidents involve drunk drivers.	Tougher laws should be passed concerning drinking and driving.
Jobs are scarce.	A good interview can land a job.
My doctor told me to lose weight.	I'm following three rules to take off weight.

□EXERCISE 1

Which of the following are merely topics or facts, and which are thesis statements that you could explain or defend? In front of each one that is a thesis statement, write THESIS. Check your answers with those at the back of the book.

_____ 1. Cross-country skiing.

_____ 2. Getting my first bike made me feel grown up.

_____ 3. Alaska has great mineral resources.

_____ 4. Teaching my pup to heel took time and patience.

_____ 5. Developers should not be allowed near Tonto National Forest for two reasons.

_____ 6. My job gives me an ego boost.

_____ 7. How to wax a car.

_____ 8. Group therapy taught me to recognize my weaknesses and cope with them.

_____ 9. My first college course about computers confirmed my decision to major in computer science.

IV. SUPPORT YOUR THESIS WITH REASONS OR POINTS

Now you're ready to support your thesis with reasons or points. That is, you'll think of ways to convince your reader that your thesis is true. How could you convince your reader that a day of backpacking made you a confirmed backpacker? You might write

> A day of backpacking in Algonquin Park made me a confirmed back-packer. (because)°
> 1. I liked traveling without suitcases.
> 2. I liked getting out into the wilderness.
> 3. I met interesting people.

The points supporting a thesis are not always reasons. They may be examples (to make your thesis clear), steps (in a how-to-paper), descriptions (in a descriptive paper), or anecdotes (in a narrative paper). Whatever they are, they should convince your reader that your thesis is true for you.

□EXERCISE 2

Add supporting points (sentences) to these thesis statements.

I've decided not to quit college.

            1.

(reasons)   2.

            3.

Our house is a madhouse when we're leaving on a trip.

            1.

            2.

(examples)

            3.

            4.

To increase your vocabulary, you need to take three steps.

            1.

(steps)   2.

            3.

° Sometimes if you imagine a "because" at the end of your thesis statement, it will help you write your reasons clearly and in parallel form.

Learning to write a good thesis statement with supporting points is perhaps the most important thing you can learn in this course. Most writing problems are not really *writing* problems but *thinking* problems. Whether you're writing a term paper or merely an answer to a test question, working out a thesis statement is always the best way to organize your thoughts. If you take enough time to think, you'll be able to write a clear thesis statement with supporting points. And if you have a clear thesis statement with supporting points, organizing your paper won't be difficult.

Assignment 3   Two Thesis Statements with Supporting Points

Think of some decision you're trying to make. Are you wondering what major to choose, whether to drop out of college for a time, whether to give up smoking, whether to try out for the next dramatic production? Think of a decision that really matters to you. Only then will you be able to write something others will care to read. When you've decided on a topic, write a thesis statement for *each side*. For example, if you're wondering whether to major in physical education or in business, you would write

I've decided to major in physical education.
I've decided to major in business.

These statements now need to be supported with reasons. You might write

I've decided to major in physical education. (because)
    1. My real interest is in sports.
    2. I'd like to influence kids.
    3. I'll be able to get a job either as a teacher or as a coach.

I've decided to major in business. (because)
    1. Age won't disqualify me later.
    2. I'll have more job opportunities.
    3. I'll make my living in business and keep sports for a hobby.

Three reasons usually work well, but you could have two or four. Be sure all your reasons are sentences.

Now write your two thesis statements for the two sides of the decision you are trying to make, and under them write your supporting reasons.

I've decided _____

    1.

    2.

    3.

I've decided _____

    1.

    2.

    3.

Eventually you'll write a paper on one of the two sides, but first we must consider two problems: how to organize a paper and how to organize a paragraph.

V. ORGANIZE YOUR PAPER FROM YOUR THESIS

Once you have worked out a good thesis with supporting points, organizing your paper will be easy.

First you need an introductory paragraph. It should catch your reader's interest and should either include or suggest your thesis statement. It may also list the supporting points, but usually it's more effective to let them unfold paragraph by paragraph rather than to give them all away in your introduction. Even if your supporting points don't appear in your introduction, your reader will easily spot them later if your paper is clearly organized.

Your second paragraph will present your first supporting point—everything about it and nothing more.

Your next paragraph will be about your second supporting point—all about it and nothing more.

Each additional paragraph will develop another supporting point.

Finally you'll need a brief concluding paragraph. In a short paper it isn't necessary to restate all your points. Even a single clincher sentence to round out the paper may be sufficient.

Paragraph 1. Introduction arousing your reader's interest and indicating your thesis

Paragraph 2. First supporting point

Paragraph 3. Second supporting point

Additional paragraphs for additional supporting points

Concluding paragraph

Learning to write this kind of paper will teach you to write logically. Then when you're ready to write a longer paper, you'll be able to organize it easily.

Here are the introductory and concluding paragraphs from a student paper. Note that the introductory paragraph arouses the reader's interest and suggests the thesis statement. And the brief concluding paragraph simply ties the whole paper together.

Introductory paragraph When we finally decided to turn off the TV for good on school days, we had a revolution. Our two youngsters—seven and nine—staged a protest so violent that it would have been worthy of any war-torn country. For two weeks our house was in a state of siege. Then three things happened.

(The writer tells in three paragraphs the changes in attitudes that took place.)

Concluding paragraph The finale to our drama came yesterday. I had turned the TV on in midafternoon to get the weather but had been called to the phone and had forgotten to turn it off. When our youngsters rushed in after school, they stopped still at the front door. Then Kristin walked slowly into the living room and turned off the TV.

VI. ORGANIZE EACH PARAGRAPH

Organizing a paragraph is easy because it's organized just the way an entire paper is. Here's the way you learned to organize a paper:

Thesis: stated or suggested in introductory paragraph.
First supporting point
Second supporting point
Additional supporting points
Concluding paragraph

And here's the way to organize a paragraph:

Topic sentence
First supporting detail or example
Second supporting detail or example
Additional supporting details or examples
Concluding sentence if needed

You should have at least two or three points to support your topic sentence. If you find that you have little to say after writing the topic sentence, ask yourself what details or examples will make your reader see that the topic sentence is true for you.

The topic sentence doesn't have to be the first sentence in the paragraph. It may come at the end or even in the middle, but having it first is the most common way and the way we'll use in the materials that follow.

Each paragraph should contain only one main idea, and no detail or example should be allowed to creep into the paragraph if it doesn't support the topic sentence. Note how the following paragraph is organized.

Driving along some of my favorite country roads last Sunday, I was glad to see that most of the roadsides had not been mowed and thus remained a haven for birds and small animals as well as an encouraging place for wildflowers. The black-eyed Susans were plentiful among the white-flowered fleabanes and Queen Anne's lace. I even saw a few plants from the endangered species list. As I approached Troublesome Creek, several quail were in the road and were reluctant to make way for my car. It was plain that it was their territory and that I was an intruder. Then a squirrel raced across the road, and some baby rabbits hopped about among the low bushes. After a while I returned to the highway and to the monotonous border of miles and miles of mowed grass.

The rather long topic sentence states that unmowed roadsides are a haven for birds, small animals, and plants. Then abundant details follow, and the final clincher sentence adds emphasis to the topic sentence.

Transition Expressions

Transition expressions within a paragraph help the reader move from one detail or example to the next.

□EXERCISE 3

Here are some transition expressions that would make the following paragraph read more smoothly. In each blank in the paragraph write the transition expression you think appropriate. Check your answers with those at the back of the book.

Also

In the first place

Then too

Therefore

I've made up my mind to try out for the marching band this fall. _____, two of my best friends are in the band and are begging me to try out. _____, I've been wanting to try out for a couple of years but have simply never had the nerve. _____, my parents keep asking me why I don't try out. _____ this seems like the time to do it. If I'm lucky enough to make it, I'll gain confidence, and even if I don't make it, just trying out will be a good experience. So I'm practicing hard, and come Tuesday evening, I'll be out there tooting my horn.

Transition expressions are also important throughout a paper. They help a reader to move from one supporting point to the next. It is often a good idea to start each supporting paragraph in a paper with a transition expression.

There are transitions to show addition:

Also
Furthermore
Another (example, point, etc. . .)
Then too

There are transitions to show sequence:

First	One reason	One example
Secondly	Another reason	Another example
Finally	Most importantly	

There are transitions to show contrast:

On the other hand
However

The easiest and most natural way to practice writing transitions is to write them as part of a paper. You'll have an opportunity to practice writing transitions in the assignments that follow.

Assignment 4   A Decision I Have Made

Return to the two thesis statements with supporting points that you wrote concerning a decision you are trying to make (Assignment 3, pp. 196–197). Choose one to write about. Even if your mind is not really made up, you must focus on one side if your paper is to be effective.

Here's a student paper on this assignment. Note that the first paragraph suggests but doesn't state the thesis. The second paragraph gives the first reason for the decision. The third paragraph gives the second reason. And the final paragraph is merely a sentence underscoring the decision.

CURTAIN TIME

All my life I assumed I was going to be a doctor. It was just taken for granted in our family that I'd follow in my dad's footsteps. I took science courses in high school, and I had no doubts. But then last fall I came to college, and college has changed everything.

First of all, a psychology course made me do some hard thinking about my interests, and after a long time I came to the conclusion that the medical world isn't for me. Oh, I know the advantages. If I became a doctor, I'd be helping people just as my father does. It would be a good life, a life I could be proud of. But somehow that just isn't where my interests lie. I can't get excited about it. And this spring, for the first time, I've had the guts to admit it.

Furthermore, I've now found out what I really do want to do. Last fall I had a small part in the play *I Never Sang for My Father,* and I had more fun than I've had in years. Not only did I enjoy doing my little part well, but I liked helping move scenery, watching the makeup artists, and seeing everything that went on backstage. Then this spring I had a great opportunity. I got to play the Stage Manager in *Our Town.* And that did it! Never before had I felt so exhilarated. Never before had I been so completely wrapped up in what I was doing. And at the end of our first evening's performance, I knew that the theater is the life for me. Oh, I know I won't be a Dustin Hoffman or an Al Pacino. In fact I'm not even sure whether I want to act or to produce, but I know I want to be part of the theater world.

Now all I live for is to hear that call—"Curtain Time."

Now write your paper, giving enough specific details in each supporting paragraph to convince your reader that you've made the right decision.

VII. WRITE AND REWRITE

If possible, write your paper several days before it's due. Let it sit for a day. When you reread it, you'll see ways to improve it. After rewriting it, put it away for another day, and try again to improve it.

Great writers don't just sit down and write their books in a first draft. They write and rewrite. Hemingway said, "I wrote the ending to *A Farewell to Arms,* the last page of it, thirty-nine times before I was satisfied." And Leo Tolstoy wrote, "I can't understand how anyone can write without rewriting everything over and over again."

Don't call any paper finished until you have worked through it several times. REWRITING IS THE BEST WAY TO LEARN TO WRITE.

Assignment 5   An Achievement

Describe some achievement you are proud of. It might be something from your childhood or something recent. Perhaps no one knows about it. Your thesis statement might have as supporting points the steps you took to achieve what you did or the reasons you are proud of your accomplishment.

Write your paper and then put it aside.

Here is a student paper on this assignment, a second draft. Note how the writer has improved the first draft by

1. Crossing out unnecessary words or expressions.
2. Adding more specific words or details.

Can you see why each change was made? In the left-hand margin, write the reason you think the writer made the change. Analyzing the reasons for the changes will help you improve your own writing.

MY GO-CART

I remember the day I finished my go-cart, which is what kids' racing cars were called when I was growing up. I'd been working on it for weeks after school and on weekends. ~~Every day after school I could hardly wait to get my clothes changed and get out to the garage~~. I had built the frame in the shop at school and had got an old gas lawnmower engine from ~~my~~ our neighbor. Then I bought *the wheels and/parts* all the other ~~pieces~~ for it at junk stores and an automotive parts place.

It was my project, my design, and my construction. It felt great just to look at it, all finished and ready to go. I pushed it out onto the driveway with a little help from my friends. It felt good to sit in the seat and put my feet on the pedals. The excitement about that first ride was contagious; everyone was talking and helping, ~~and all. We did a last minute final check on it and~~ I started the engine, and then I took off. What a great sensation, moving along under the power of my own machine! I sped up, slowed down, turned left, turned right, and then braked, and it all worked! I had a great feeling as I circled back to my friends. I felt the pride of having created my own machine, and I relished the envy in my friends' eyes. We all took turns on it that afternoon and had a great time.

I've built bigger projects since then. I've even rebuilt *the engine in* my car, but I've never felt more satisfaction than on that first day with my go-cart.

Now reread your paper on An Achievement and see what improvements you can make before you copy it in final form.

Here's a checklist of questions to ask yourself as you begin to rewrite:

1. Will my introductory paragraph make my reader want to read further?
2. Does each paragraph support my thesis statement?
3. Does each paragraph contain only one main idea?
4. Do I have enough specific details in each paragraph to support the topic sentence, and are all the details relevant?
5. Does my concluding paragraph sum up my paper in a persuasive way?
6. Have I checked all questionable spellings?
7. Is my punctuation correct?

VIII. PROOFREAD ALOUD

Finally, read your finished paper ALOUD. If you read it silently, you're sure to miss some errors. Read it aloud slowly, word by word, to catch omitted words and errors in spelling and punctuation. Make it a rule to read each of your papers **aloud** before handing it in.

As you do the following assignments, be sure to take each of the EIGHT STEPS TO BETTER WRITING.

Assignment 6   A Backward Look

Now that you're in college, you can look back on your high school years more realistically. How do you now feel about the way your parents treated you during those years? Do you think, "Thanks, Mom and Dad, for all your did," or do you think, "Why didn't you . . . ?" Do some free writing to clarify your thoughts. Then write a thesis statement giving your present thinking. Write a short paper on the subject giving the reasons for your attitude, and remember that it's specific examples that make a paper come alive.

Assignment 7   Getting Along with Someone

Write down the name of someone you have trouble getting along with. You may make up a name, but have a real person in mind. Write a thesis statement listing ways in which you wish that person would change so that the two of you could get along better.

As we all know, however, it's difficult to get someone else to change. Therefore now write a thesis statement listing ways in which *you* could change to make the relationship better. Perhaps you are saying, "Impossible." Think. There are always ways. Think until you have a realistic, possible thesis statement for your paper. This paper will be harder to write than if you wrote about how the other person should change, but it will teach you more about writing. Remember that learning to write is learning to think.

Assignment 8   How to Do Something

Nothing will get rid of the clutter in your writing like writing a "how to" paper. Every sentence will have to be clear and to the point.

Write a short paper telling someone how to do something—for example, how to paint a table, how to choose a stereo system, how to put a three-year-old to bed, how to make a piece of costume jewelry, or how to change the oil in a car.

First you'll need an introductory paragraph—a sentence will do—to interest your reader, then a step-by-step explanation, and finally a concluding paragraph, which again may be just one sentence. You may want to add some humor to your introduction or conclusion to make your paper more interesting.

Assignment 9   Choosing a Career

What career are you considering? Be specific. Rather than saying Teaching, say Teaching High School Math. Give the reasons that make you think you'd like that career. If you have no idea what you want to do, simply choose any likely possibility.

Assignment 10   A Quotation

Look through the quotations on pages 167–173 and pick one that especially appeals to you, either because you have found it true in your own experience or because you know you should follow its advice. Write a thesis statement explaining your reaction to the quotation, and back up your thesis with reasons or examples.

Assignment 11   A Surprise

What has surprised you most since coming to college? It might be a surprise about social life, about the attitude of professors, or about the attitude of students. Just how is college different from what you thought it would be? After you have done some free writing and limited your topic, work out a good thesis statement, giving two or three examples to support your opinion.

Assignment 12   Five Minutes

If you could live over again any five minutes of your life, what five minutes would you choose? Why?

Assignment 13　My Opinion on a Current Problem

Choose one of the problems below and present your arguments for one side. Write a carefully thought-out thesis statement, supported by reasons, before you begin your paper. In your introduction or conclusion you may want to mention briefly the reasons you can see for the opposite side.

A. As an admissions officer of your college, you have only one space left in the freshman class for the coming fall, and you are trying to decide between two applicants. One is a straight B student who has won honors in high school debate and has participated in dramatics. The other is a minority student from a disadvantaged background who has only a D average but who lettered in two high school sports. The college needs promising athletes in those two sports and also is trying to increase its proportion of minority students. Which student will you admit and why?

B. The noted historian Henry Steele Commager writes that America is the land of the immigrant, that all of us are immigrants or the descendants of immigrants, that thousands of victims of repression have found refuge in our land and contributed to our cultural and scientific wealth, that our record of welcome to immigrants is one in which we can rejoice.

Now a boatload of people from a war-torn country has landed illegally on a U.S. shore. The people are afraid for their lives and are asking for asylum. Some U.S. citizens, however, say we have too many illegal aliens already and that our land is plagued with unemployment. If you were on the congressional committee to make the decision, what would your response be and why?

C. The college bookstore, where you work part-time, is losing a lot of money to shoplifters and has asked all employees to be on the watch and to report any suspect. This morning you happen to notice a friend of yours trying on a T-shirt on the opposite side of the store. Then, as you are watching, he slips his jacket over the T-shirt and goes out the door. What should you do? The problem is complicated by the fact that he has twice befriended you—once by standing up for you when you were falsely accused in an athletic tangle and once by taking time to talk you out of quitting college. You feel indebted to him, and yet you feel an obligation to your employer and a desire to take a stand for honesty. What are you going to do? As you are thinking all this, the manager steps up to you and says, "I saw you watching that student. Did he swipe that T-shirt?" What will you say?

WRITING A SUMMARY

A good way to learn to write concisely is to write 100-word summaries. Writing 100 words sounds easy, but actually it isn't. Writing 200- or 300- or 500-word summaries isn't too difficult, but condensing all the main ideas of an essay or article into 100 words is a time-consuming task—not to be undertaken in the last hour before class. If you work at writing summaries conscientiously, you'll improve both your reading and your writing. You'll improve your reading by learning to spot main ideas and your writing by learning to construct a concise, clear, smooth paragraph. Furthermore, your skills will carry over into your reading and writing for other courses.

Assignment 14   A 100-Word Summary

Your aim in writing your summary should be to give someone who has not read the article a clear idea of it. First read the article, and then follow the instructions given after it. Difficult words are defined in the margin.

Novel Ending for Book Bugs
Noel Vietmeyer

Apparently, loud talkers are not the only pests loitering in the nation's libraries. At Yale University, librarians discovered not long ago, some unidentified insects had made mincemeat out of a priceless book collection.

loitering—remaining in an area for no obvious reason

An alumnus had donated a set of illuminated medieval manuscripts to the university after buying them from an ancient monastery in southern Italy. The manuscripts, which had been stored in an underground vault for centuries, were crawling with millions of strange, wingless insects. "They had started from the spines, and were eating into the texts," recalls a Yale professor. "There were so many grubs that those fabulous books were turning into lace doilies."

illuminated—decorated with brilliant colors

spine—the backbone of a book

Yale's problem, though severe, was not unique. A whole menagerie of pests—moths, cockroaches, booklice, silverfish, termites and bookmites— thrives in library books around the world. Insects with a less literary bent also infest records and

bent—a strong interest

other papers in town halls, administration buildings, warehouses, even people's homes. . . .

Such pests have been under siege by exterminators for years. Until World War II, the preferred treatment was cyanide—which, unfortunately, is also poisonous to humans. Organic pesticides, commonly used in libraries today, may pose health hazards of their own, especially in enclosed areas. Some libraries, researchers have found, contain alarming levels of pesticide residue.

When Yale officials were faced with the task of debugging their rare books, they couldn't even consider using chemicals. The insects were deep inside the pages, where fumes could damage the fragile paper or change the colors in the illuminations. In desperation, the librarians turned to Charles Remington, head of the department of entomology at Yale.

entomology—a branch of zoology that deals with insects

"We don't usually do that kind of research," says Remington. Nevertheless, the scientist went to work. . . .

Operating on a hunch, Remington tried freezing several of the insects. After a day and a half on ice, they were out cold—killed by the low temperatures. Encouraged, the entomologist and the librarians wrapped every one of the precious Italian books in a plastic freezer bag and commandeered a deep freeze in a campus dining hall. Then they froze the volumes for three days at minus 40 degrees Fahrenheit. A later inspection showed the embattled books to be completely bug free.

commandeer—to take forcible possession of

Since then, Yale has installed a large, walk-through freezer in the library and put its entire collection of more than 30,000 rare books and documents on ice. Now, the technique is catching on elsewhere. In Illinois, a company has been established to supply libraries with book freezers. Yale's music department recently froze an infested Stradivarius violin. . . .

"Freezing is intolerable for most life forms," observes Remington. "For infestations on things not living, it's the perfect pest control."

A good way to begin a summary of an article is to figure out the thesis statement, the main idea the author wants to get across to the reader. Write that idea down now BEFORE READING FURTHER.

How honest are you with yourself? Did you write that thesis statement? If you didn't, WRITE IT NOW before you read further.

You probably wrote something like this: *Book bugs have infested libraries for years, but now a solution has been found.*

Using that thesis statement as your first sentence, summarize the article by choosing the most important points. Your first draft may be 150 words or more. Now cut it down by including only essential points and by getting rid of wordiness. Keep within the 100-word limit. You may have a few words less but not one word more. (And every word counts—even *a, and,* and *the.*) By forcing yourself to keep within the 100 words, you'll get to the kernel of the author's thought and understand the article better.

When you have written the best summary you can, then, *and only then,* compare it with the summary on page 259. If you look at the model sooner, you'll cheat yourself of the opportunity to learn to write summaries because once you read the model, it will be almost impossible not to make yours similar. So do your own thinking and writing, and *then* compare.

Even though your summary is different from the model, it may be just as good. If you're not sure how yours compares, ask yourself these questions:

Did I include as many important ideas?
Did I omit all unnecessary words?
Does my summary read as smoothly?
Would someone who had not read the article get a clear idea of it from
    my summary?

Assignment 15   A 100-Word Summary

After you read this concise article, you may wonder how you can condense it more, but you can. Turn it into a 100-word summary that will include just the most essential parts—the parts you would like to keep in your mind forever.

The Incredible Machine
(A condensed version of a National Geographic Society videotape)

Scientists have said that the human body is made up of about two-thirds water, plus carbon, calcium, and a few other chemicals—all worth about five dollars. But the body performs amazing feats of engineering, chemistry, and physics that no machine designed by humans can duplicate.

For example, the heart—merely the size of a fist and weighing less than a pound—is a marvel of mechanical performance. Beating seventy times a minute, it pumps two thousand gallons of blood a day and fifty-five million gallons in a lifetime.

Blood—the river of life—journeys endlessly through sixty thousand miles of blood vessels. Oxygen, water, and nutrients are delivered to every cell, and waste products are collected. A complete tour—out from the heart and back—takes less than a minute.

The stomach churns food and mixes it with enzymes and acid. In normal digestion the stomach produces hydrochloric acid strong enough to burn a hole in a rug, but it protects itself with a glistening layer of mucous.

Of the body's 206 bones, more than half are in the hands and feet. The unique engineering design of the human body reaches its apex in the hand. Twenty-five joints give it fifty-eight distinctly different motions and make it the most versatile instrument on earth.

All we ever see of one another—skin and hair—is dead. Our skin is constantly growing from within, creating new cells that push their way outward, then die near the surface. Our skin perspires constantly. Even when we are not exerting, we perspire between one and two pints of water a day.

The human body, an incredible machine.

Assignment 16   A 100-Word Summary

First read this article and note how it's organized. By the time you figure out the thesis statement and the points under the thesis statement,
you'll be well on your way to writing your summary. Since it isn't necessary to include examples, your summary will probably require fewer than
100 words.

Digging for Roots

Why is a hippopotamus called a hippopotamus? How did daises get
their name? Why is an open-air fire called a bonfire? And how did that
little dog running down the street come to be called a terrier? Where did
names come from anyway? Most names didn't just happen. They grew
from roots. And when you uncover their roots, you'll often find interesting stories.

It was no accident that a hippopotamus was named hippopotamus. The
early Greeks thought the big animal they saw in rivers looked a bit like a
fat horse, so they called it a river horse (HIPP *horse*, POTAMOS *river*).
In early England people called that little flower with the white petals and
a large yellow center a DAY'S EYE or **daisy.** In Europe in the Middle
Ages, during times of war or plague, corpses were piled up and burned together in a BONE FIRE. Eventually any open-air fire came to be called
a bonfire or **bonfire.** That active little **terrier** running down the street
got its name from the Latin root TERR *(earth)* because it was originally a
hunting dog that dug in the earth to get small animals out of their bur-
rows. Many such stories can be found in your dictionary. Look for the material in square brackets either just before or just after the definition.
Such words as *gymnasium, salary, companion,* and *curfew* are fun to look
up because they have interesting derivations.

But digging for word roots can do more than unearth entertaining stories. It's the quickest way to improve your vocabulary.

First, looking up the roots of a word will help you remember its meaning. For example, you might find it difficult to remember a big word like
antediluvian if you merely looked up its meaning. But if you look up its
roots, you won't easily forget it. It is made up of ANTE *(before)* and
DILUVIUM *(flood)* and means "before the flood" described in the
Bible. If something was in existence "before the flood," it must be very
old or primitive. Therefore if you want to exaggerate the age of something
you can call it antediluvian. A farmer without a tractor or an office without a computer would be using antediluvian methods. And if you are trying to convince someone—or yourself—that your car is old enough to turn
in on a new model, you can call it antediluvian.

Adapted from *The Least You Should Know about Vocabulary Building,* by Teresa Ferster
Glazier, Harcourt Brace, 1993.

Second, learning the roots of a word will not only help you remember its meaning but will also help you learn other words containing the same root. For example, if you learn that **philanthropist** is made up of PHIL *(to love)* and ANTHROP *(human being)*, then you've learned not only that a philanthropist is a lover or benefactor of human beings, but you have a clue to some seventy other words beginning with PHIL and to more than sixty others beginning with ANTHROP. *Webster's Third New International Dictionary* lists that many words beginning with those two roots.

Since you now know that PHIL means *to love*, you'll readily see that philharmonic means "love of harmony"—an appropriate name for a symphony orchestra. Philadelphia (ADELPH brother) is the city of "brotherly love"; a bibliophile (BIBL *book*) is a "lover (or collector) of books"; and anyone named Philip (PHIL to love HIPP horse) is a lover of horses.

Third, learning word roots will do something more than help you learn new words. It will give more meaning to words you already know. **Escape,** for example, comes from EX *(out)* and CAP *(cape)* and originally meant to get "out of one's cape." Perhaps while a jailer was holding a prisoner by his cape, the prisoner got "out of his cape" and got free. He had escaped. **Precocious** (PRE *before,* COCT *to cook*) originally meant "cooked before time." Therefore if you have a precocious child, the child has been "cooked before time" or has matured earlier than most children.

So dig for roots. Enjoy their stories. Add to your vocabulary. And find more meaning in words you already know.

Assignment 17   A 100-Word Summary

Write a 100-word summary of this article, which takes an unusual view of immigrants.

Immigrants in Vancouver

Immigration has become a problem in many countries but especially in the Province of British Columbia in Canada. There the geographical position of Vancouver makes that city the gateway for immigrants from Hong Kong and the rest of Asia.

The citizens of Vancouver have been loath to express their worries, but gradually they are admitting concern over the changes that have taken place. They are wondering, for example, whether their children will get a good education since the schools are now geared to teaching children whose main need is to learn English as a second language.

loath—reluctant

geared—adjusted

But even those who dislike some aspects of immigration have to admit that it is largely responsible for the city's buoyant economy.

buoyant—having a tendency to rise or float

The Lieutenant Governor of British Columbia, David See-Chai Lam, is one of Canada's most successful immigrants. He came to Vancouver from Hong Kong in 1957 and made a fortune in real estate. Then he was appointed Lieutenant Governor of the province and now is trying to increase understanding between established Canadians and new arrivals. Lam says he would like Canada to celebrate its immigrants and not just tolerate them. He says his greatest contribution to Canada has been as a symbol of change. That symbol is a person of the Chinese race like himself occupying Vancouver's most important residence.

Many immigrants have been taken into Canadian life, with the House of Commons including MPs from China, Japan, India, the Philippines, and the East Indies. One person in the City Council said, "Vancouver has always accepted waves of immigrants and has always been enriched by them."

WRITING AN APPLICATION

Assignment 18   A Letter of Application

You may not need to do much writing in the career you have chosen, but almost certainly you will at some time need to write a letter of application. Write a letter of application now, either for a job this coming summer or for a job you might want to apply for after you finish college. Follow the form given here.

```
500 West Adams Street
Macomb, IL 61455
February 2, 1996

Mr. John Witkowski, Director
Chicago Park District
425 East McFetridge Drive
Chicago, IL 60605

Dear Mr. Witkowski:

I have seen your ad in the Chicago Tribune for helpers
in the Park District Recreation Department for the
coming summer. I would like to be considered for a
position.

I am a freshman at Western Illinois University and
am majoring in special education. For two summers I
have worked with children who are physically and
mentally disabled and have found the work very
rewarding. Therefore I would be particularly pleased
if I could work with such children.

I have listed my training and experience on the
enclosed personal data sheet, and I will be glad to
come for an interview at your convenience.


Sincerely,



Jane Keeler
```

WRITING AN EVALUATION

Assignment 19   An Evaluation of My Performance

Do five minutes of free writing in preparation for writing a short paper on your performance in this course. Don't evaluate the course—it may have been bad or good—but simply evaluate how you performed. Although you may need to mention some weakness or strength of the course, the emphasis should be on how you reacted to that weakness or strength.

Don't be afraid to be honest. This isn't an occasion for apple-polishing. If you've gained little, you'll write a better paper by saying so than by trying to make up phony gains. Someone who has gained little may write a better paper than someone who has gained much. How well the paper is organized and whether there are plenty of specific examples will determine the effectiveness of the paper.

Before starting your paper, write your thesis statement, listing your supporting points. If you've made gains, list the kinds—gain in writing skill, gain in confidence, gain in study habits. . . . Or, if you've gained little, list the reasons why—lack of time, lack of interest, getting off to a bad start. . . .

Since no one will have all gains or all losses in any course, you may want to include in your introduction or conclusion a sentence about the other side.

Answers

Answers

Words Often Confused (p. 11)

EXERCISE 1

1. new, effect
2. It's, accept, advice, an
3. course
4. conscious, new
5. complement, already
6. chose, new
7. choose
8. our
9. break
10. feel, do, it's, have

EXERCISE 2

1. knew, an
2. course
3. an
4. desert
5. knew
6. our
7. no, compliment
8. chose
9. are
10. it's

EXERCISE 3

1. chose, except
2. new, already
3. an, break, here
4. It's
5. doesn't
6. advice
7. It's
8. forth, are
9. course, dessert
10. an

EXERCISE 4

1. chose
2. an
3. effect, course
4. The sentence is correct.
5. hear
6. are
7. do
8. hear
9. clothes, knew, no
10. do, have

EXERCISE 5

1. an, our
2. course, already, knew, it's
3. conscious, its
4. have, it's, an
5. knew
6. know, it's
7. an
8. no
9. know, does
10. chose, course, already

EXERCISE 6

1. an
2. It's
3. effect
4. knew, except, are
5. are

6. break
7. an
8. our
9. are, are
10. course

EXERCISE 7

1. course
2. new
3. or
4. are
5. or, course

6. except
7. do
8. new
9. The sentence is correct.
10. its

EXERCISE 8

1. hear, new
2. new, already
3. know
4. are, an, effect
5. conscious, an, effect, our

6. It's
7. effect
8. knew
9. are
10. does

More Words Often Confused (p. 19)

EXERCISE 1

1. knew, right, here
2. conscious, course, are
3. they're, too
4. there
5. than

6. course, they're
7. too
8. hear
9. through
10. whether

EXERCISE 2

1. an
2. It's, new
3. there
4. are, courses
5. It's

6. course, there, their
7. than
8. loose, weather, whether
9. their
10. than

EXERCISE 3

1. There, right
2. principal, through
3. here
4. there
5. quiet

6. its, its
7. Where
8. here
9. do
10. Then, There

EXERCISE 4

1. or, are
2. The sentence is correct.
3. an
4. were, then, its
5. then

6. are
7. does
8. or, it's
9. its
10. were, past, are

EXERCISE 5

1. weather
2. our
3. weather
4. right, our
5. were

6. right
7. Then, There
8. The sentence is correct.
9. Then
10. were, our

EXERCISE 6

1. course
2. know, there, our
3. an
4. where, there, an, a
5. there, are

6. are
7. are, than, past
8. two
9. there, are
10. you're, than

EXERCISE 7

1. knew, than, our
2. an, it's
3. It's, than, an
4. than
5. Its

6. except
7. are
8. already, are, an
9. are, their
10. course, does, conscious

EXERCISE 8

1. an, knew
2. Its, than, have
3. are
4. are
5. There, an

6. quite
7. where, it's
8. an, past, course
9. there
10. do, there

EXERCISE 9

1. know, whether
2. principal, course, does
3. It's, our, write
4. our
5. quite

6. or
7. course, than
8. know
9. know, where
10. quite, through

EXERCISE 10

1. Our, an
2. There, no
3. quiet, its
4. past, where
5. then, its

6. there, through
7. have, fill
8. know, it's
9. Its, its, than
10. hear, quite

Use of Apostrophe: Contractions (p. 27)

EXERCISE 1

1. I've
2. They're, can't
3. They've
4. The sentence is correct.
5. it's

6. they're
7. can't, aren't
8. it's
9. aren't
10. They're

EXERCISE 2

1. didn't, haven't
2. I've
3. I've, weren't
4. hadn't
5. The sentence is correct.

6. wasn't
7. weren't
8. The sentence is correct.
9. didn't
10. hasn't

EXERCISE 3

1. Haven't
2. I've
3. aren't, they're
4. aren't, they're
5. There's

6. you've, you'll
7. they're
8. It's
9. It's
10. they're

EXERCISE 4

1. I've, can't, that's
2. There's, didn't
3. I'll
4. It's
5. I'd

6. It's
7. there's
8. You'll, you'll
9. It's, I'm
10. I'm

EXERCISE 5

1. I'm, it's
2. I'd, it's
3. I've, they're
4. I've
5. I'm, don't

6. It's, I've
7. I've
8. I'm, I'm
9. It's, what's
10. I've, can't

EXERCISE 6

1. There's, you've
2. weren't
3. who's
4. The sentence is correct.
5. I'm, I've

6. The sentence is correct.
7. isn't, who's
8. who's
9. It's
10. I'm

EXERCISE 7

1. I've, didn't
2. It's
3. didn't
4. hadn't
5. didn't

6. didn't
7. wasn't, didn't
8. It's, wouldn't
9. aren't
10. I'll

EXERCISE 8

1. I've
2. I've
3. I'd
4. I've, they're
5. they're

6. They're
7. they're
8. The sentence is correct.
9. won't
10. The sentence is correct.

EXERCISE 9

1. it's, eyes
2. The sentence is correct.
3. doesn't
4. The sentence is correct.
5. The sentence is correct.

6. it's, that's
7. It's
8. The sentence is correct.
9. they're
10. The sentence is correct.

EXERCISE 10

1. it's, it's
2. The sentence is correct.
3. The sentence is correct.
4. It's
5. The sentence is correct.

6. can't
7. aren't, it's
8. doesn't
9. The sentence is correct.
10. she's

Use of Apostrophe: Possessives (p. 36)

EXERCISE 1

1. man's
2. The sentence is correct.
3. Kimberly's, Sarah's
4. Alfredo's
5. The sentence is correct.
6. Everyone's
7. Bess'
8. dad's
9. somebody's
10. yesterday's

EXERCISE 2

1. everybody's
2. students'
3. person's
4. else's
5. Someone's
6. students'
7. students'
8. instructor's
9. student's
10. Everybody's

EXERCISE 3

1. Saturday's
2. everybody's
3. men's, women's
4. boys', men's
5. children's
6. niece's
7. sister's
8. parents'
9. morning's
10. people's

EXERCISE 4

1. Women's
2. president's
3. president's
4. senator's
5. Senate's
6. women's
7. women's
8. The sentence is correct.
9. anyone's
10. senator's

EXERCISE 5

1. summer's
2. year's
3. day's
4. Ben's
5. customer's
6. customers'
7. woman's
8. manager's
9. day's
10. bagger's

EXERCISE 6

1. visitor's
2. The sentence is correct.
3. People's
4. Children's
5. visitors'
6. Indians'
7. anyone's
8. country's
9. person's
10. The sentence is correct.

EXERCISE 7

1. Sally's
2. The sentence is correct.
3. The sentence is correct.
4. Butterflies'
5. Butterflies'

6. butterfly's
7. butterflies', butterflies'
8. butterflies', rodents', snakes'
9. The sentence is correct.
10. butterfly's

EXERCISE 8

1. summer's
2. Utah's
3. mom's
4. The sentence is correct.
5. Mom's

6. family's
7. Everybody's
8. dad's
9. The sentence is correct.
10. world's

EXERCISE 9

1. Everybody's
2. The sentence is correct.
3. person's
4. person's
5. Kent's, brother's

6. Amanda's, sister's
7. day's
8. week's
9. evening's
10. Everyone's

EXERCISE 10

1. person's
2. person's
3. The sentence is correct.
4. creature's
5. The sentence is correct.

6. fly's
7. The sentence is correct.
8. fly's
9. Mosquitoes'
10. people's

Review of Contractions and Possessives (p. 40)

EXERCISE 1

1. I've, I've
2. I'd, don't
3. plant's, isn't
4. it's
5. plant's

6. The sentence is correct.
7. The sentence is correct.
8. That's, I'd, don't
9. they're, they're
10. they're

EXERCISE 2

1. I've, I've
2. body's
3. couldn't, there's
4. it's (first one)
5. The sentence is correct.

6. you'd
7. couldn't, you'd
8. planet's, you'd
9. gravity's, you'd
10. There's

Doubling a Final Consonant (p. 44)

EXERCISE 1

1. dropping
2. drooping
3. compelling
4. mopping
5. planning
6. hopping
7. beginning
8. knitting
9. marking
10. creeping

EXERCISE 2

1. offering
2. bragging
3. honoring
4. benefiting
5. loafing
6. nailing
7. omitting
8. occurring
9. shopping
10. interrupting

EXERCISE 3

1. referring
2. happening
3. submitting
4. interpreting
5. preferring
6. excelling
7. wrapping
8. stopping
9. wedding
10. screaming

EXERCISE 4

1. abandoning
2. differing
3. conferring
4. weeding
5. subtracting
6. streaming
7. expelling
8. missing
9. getting
10. stressing

EXERCISE 5

1. hindering
2. prohibiting
3. warring
4. suffering
5. pinning
6. trusting
7. sipping
8. flopping
9. reaping
10. carting

Progress Test (p. 45)

1. B
2. B
3. B
4. A
5. B
6. A
7. B
8. B
9. A
10. A
11. B
12. B
13. B
14. A
15. B

Subjects and Verbs (p. 56)

EXERCISE 1

1. trees are
2. They grow
3. They are
4. Redwoods grow
5. They resist
6. bark resists
7. trees live
8. Some are
9. Many were
10. wood varies

EXERCISE 2

1. we saw
2. fire swept
3. smoke was
4. flames were
5. flames rose
6. motorist saw
7. he alerted
8. fighters spread
9. They had
10. cabin burned

EXERCISE 3

1. cloud was
2. lizard darted
3. Locusts swarmed
4. sound grew
5. we saw
6. wind shifted
7. mountains rose
8. sun sank
9. prairie became
10. We were

EXERCISE 4

1. koala is
2. It is
3. koala looks
4. animal has
5. food consists
6. forests exist
7. population dwindles
8. koala is
9. It crawls
10. koala rides

EXERCISE 5

1. state has
2. cardinal is
3. states chose
4. states are
5. bird is
6. It belongs
7. nene is
8. bird is
9. wren was
10. bird is

EXERCISE 6

1. Oceans cover
2. oceans are
3. waters join
4. they make
5. oceans are
6. fluids are
7. This is
8. oceans give
9. They send
10. clouds supply

EXERCISE 7

1. sea gives
2. one-fifth comes
3. people like
4. 30 percent live
5. sea provides
6. People like
7. Playing includes
8. Playing includes
9. divers explore
10. Others hunt

EXERCISE 8

1. I took
2. I visited
3. It contains
4. I learned
5. Seurat used
6. Picasso burned
7. Van Gogh applied
8. paintings interested
9. I bought
10. (You) try

EXERCISE 9

1. I knew
2. I read
3. It was
4. Ten to fifteen percent are
5. presidents were
6. you saw
7. Leonardo, Raphael, Holbein, and Picasso are
8. Harpo Marx and Charlie Chaplin were
9. Chaplin played
10. I have

Subjects Not in Prepositional Phrases (p. 62)

EXERCISE 1

1. One ~~of the latest fads on college campuses~~ is juggling.

2. The art ~~of juggling~~ is inexpensive and easy to learn.

3. ~~At MIT~~ jugglers pass clubs ~~in complicated patterns~~.

4. ~~At the Williams College commencement in 1984,~~ a graduate accepted his diploma.

5. Then he lit three torches ~~for a spectacular juggling display for the audience~~.

6. The members ~~of the International Jugglers Association~~ number almost three thousand.

7. Eighty percent ~~of the jugglers~~ are amateurs.

8. ~~In Tonga~~ women jugglers keep seven limes or green tui tui nuts airborne.

9. A Guinness record ~~for juggled objects~~ is eleven rings ~~in motion by a juggler in Russia in 1973~~.

10. Anthony Gott holds a Guinness record ~~for juggling seven flaming torches in 1989~~.

EXERCISE 2

1. Hibernation differs ~~from sleep~~.
2. ~~In sleep~~ animals merely relax.
3. ~~In hibernation~~, however, their life almost stops.
4. The breathing ~~of the animals~~ becomes very slow.
5. The beating ~~of their hearts~~ becomes irregular.
6. ~~During hibernation~~, a woodchuck's body is only a little warmer than the air ~~in its burrow~~.
7. Some kinds ~~of insects~~ freeze almost solid.
8. ~~In preparing for hibernation~~, mammals generally eat large amounts ~~of food~~.
9. They store the food ~~in thick layers of fat~~.
10. Groundhogs, ~~for example~~, become very plump ~~before hibernation~~.

EXERCISE 3

1. The national bird ~~of the United States~~ is the bald eagle.
2. ~~With its white head and white tail feathers~~, it is easy to identify.
3. But bald eagles are now an endangered species.
4. Cedar Glen ~~along the Mississippi River in Illinois~~ is a haven ~~for them~~.
5. An area ~~of 580 acres around Cedar Glen~~ is now one ~~of the largest eagle sanctuaries in the country~~.
6. ~~After their breeding season in the northern states and Canada~~, approximately 300 eagles gather ~~at Cedar Glen for the winter~~.
7. ~~For five or six months~~ each winter they stay ~~in this protected place~~.
8. ~~On frigid winter nights~~ the eagles perch ~~beside each other on the branches of large sycamore trees~~.

9. More bald eagles spend the winter ~~at Cedar Glen~~ than ~~at any other place in the Midwest~~.

10. Havens ~~like this~~ ensure a future ~~for our national bird~~.

EXERCISE 4

1. ~~Of all the states in the Union~~, Alaska is the largest.

2. One ~~of its most impressive features~~ is the nation's tallest mountain.

3. Alaskans call the mountain Denali, a Native American word ~~for "great one."~~

4. ~~Of all our national forests~~, Alaska has the largest—the Tongass National Forest ~~with seventeen million acres~~.

5. ~~In that forest~~ are four-hundred-year-old Sitka spruces.

6. Now the pristine beauty ~~of Alaska~~ is threatened by ~~lumbering interests and oil companies~~.

7. Loggers have already cut approximately 300,000 acres ~~of the Tongass Forest~~.

8. The lumber companies cut approximately 10,000 acres ~~of old-growth evergreens~~ each year.

9. Furthermore, oil interests want to build a new natural gas pipeline ~~for bringing gas from Prudhoe Bay to market~~.

10. It is a question ~~of providing economic growth versus protecting an invaluable wildlife reserve~~.

EXERCISE 5

1. ~~On a backpacking trip to Alaska~~, we visited Admiralty Island National Monument.

2. ~~With no changes since the end of the last Ice Age~~, the island stands ~~in its original grandeur~~.

3. ~~In the center of the island~~, rugged snowcapped peaks rise five thousand feet ~~above the magnificent forests~~.

4. The natives call the island "The Fortress of the Bears."

5. It is home ~~to approximately a thousand Alaskan brown bears or grizzlies~~.

6. ~~Along the shores~~ are <u>havens</u> ~~for young salmon and king crab~~.

7. <u>Admiralty Island</u> <u>is</u> one ~~of the few totally natural areas~~ left ~~in this country~~.

8. But now a logging <u>firm</u> <u>wants</u> to cut 23,000 acres ~~of virgin timber on the island~~ and to build a logging transfer terminal ~~on the shore~~.

9. <u>Congress</u> <u>passed</u> the Alaska Lands Act ~~in 1980~~ to protect such areas.

10. <u>It</u> often <u>takes</u> years ~~of legal battles~~, however, to halt the loggers.

EXERCISE 6

1. Last year there <u>was</u> a labor <u>dispute</u> ~~on our campus~~ here ~~in Vancouver~~.

2. The campus maintenance <u>workers</u>, ~~with the approval of their labor union~~, <u>threatened</u> to strike and to shut down the whole campus.

3. Many ~~of the students~~ <u>supported</u> the workers.

4. <u>They</u> <u>forgot</u> ~~about losing~~ their entire semester's credits.

5. Also there <u>were</u> only a few maintenance <u>workers</u> ~~in contrast to two thousand students~~.

6. <u>I</u> <u>decided</u> to write a letter ~~to the campus newspaper~~ and also one ~~to the city paper~~.

7. Then <u>I</u> <u>circulated</u> a petition ~~on campus about students' rights~~.

8. <u>I</u> <u>explained</u> the students' concern ~~about losing~~ a semester's credit.

9. Luckily the two <u>sides</u> <u>reached</u> a settlement quickly ~~with no classes disrupted~~.

10. <u>Participating</u> ~~in campus politics~~ <u>is</u> both enjoyable and worthwhile.

More about Subjects and Verbs (p. 66)

EXERCISE 1

1. library is
2. It contains, holds
3. Books, periodicals, and recordings pour
4. Three-quarters are
5. Buildings were
6. Library was
7. It is, is
8. library has
9. Maps, chart, and map are
10. employees send

EXERCISE 2

1. book is
2. volume is, was
3. papers are
4. library contains
5. pieces are

6. collection is
7. collection features
8. Library has become
9. Libraries can borrow
10. (You) Visit, take

EXERCISE 3

1. I have been reading
2. Whooping crane is
3. hundreds were
4. numbers declined
5. sites were
6. whooping cranes were

7. Canadian National Railway planned
8. Environmentalists got
9. some are being
10. hundreds can be seen

EXERCISE 4

1. One is
2. squirrel gets
3. squirrel feeds
4. squirrel feeds
5. bark is

6. animals are
7. It builds
8. it lines
9. mating occurs, litter is
10. young remain

EXERCISE 5

1. I have learned
2. I have known
3. article tells
4. urge is
5. animals and people learn

6. Monkeys play
7. animals play
8. They learn
9. Play is
10. It teaches

Correcting Run-Together Sentences (p. 71)

EXERCISE 1

1. I am writing, he is
2. He has designed, he won
3. He has designed, achievement has restored
4. complex consists, it has
5. building, courthouse are included

6. courthouse is, roof is
7. Robson Square is, it is
8. Robson Square has
9. tank is heated, cooled; buildings are heated, cooled
10. Most has been, project is

EXERCISE 2

1. Liberty. Then
2. people. They
3. The sentence is correct.
4. sheets;
5. finished. Then

6. Harbor. Thus
7. high. She
8. tablet. It
9. continents,
10. crown. I

EXERCISE 3

1. problems,
2. West. Now
3. Park,
4. natural,
5. bears,

6. well,
7. campgrounds,
8. homes,
9. dumps,
10. habits;

EXERCISE 4

1. Museum. It
2. *Louis.* Here
3. spacecraft. They
4. The sentence is correct.
5. *Workshop.* Here

6. ceiling,
7. The sentence is correct.
8. sensational;
9. The sentence is correct.
10. year. It

EXERCISE 5

1. them. I
2. *National Geographic,* and
3. "lizard." Thus
4. ago, and
5. countries, but

6. years, and
7. The sentence is correct.
8. ago, but
9. them, or
10. knows. Excavating

EXERCISE 6

1. process. A
2. parts. His
3. coast. They
4. The sentence is correct.
5. Alaska, or

6. The sentence is correct.
7. there. A
8. The sentence is correct.
9. Berlin; it
10. continues. We

EXERCISE 7

1. Last spring we were driving through Arizona and decided to see the Petrified Forest. Therefore we took the twenty-seven-mile drive through that strange landscape. Trees have turned to stone, and thousands of great stone logs lie on the ground. We learned a great deal about petrified wood and were glad for the experience. The National Park Service is preserving the area for future generations.

2. Bicycling is *the* mode of travel today. More than ten million cycles were sold in 1989, and eighty-four million cyclists are now pedaling on a regular basis. As many women as men cycle, and for the first time in history adult riders outnumber kids. Becoming popular are the long noncompetitive bicycle rides like the 495-mile "Annual Great Bicycle Ride Across Iowa" and the "Hotter 'N Hell Hundred" starting in Waco, Texas. Probably the longest ride is the "Pedal for Power" from Maine to Florida. Yes, bicycling is in.

3. A car running on a tankful of sunshine? Yes, it has happened. Students from thirty-two colleges designed their cars to capture the sun's rays; then the cars' photovoltaic cells converted the rays into electricity to run the motors. The students took part in the 1,641-mile "Sunrayce USA" from Florida to Michigan. It was the largest rally ever held for sun-powered cars. Of course the internal combustion engine won't soon be replaced by a tankful of sunshine, but the Sunrayce did point the way to more aerodynamic car designs for saving fuel.

Correcting Fragments (p. 78)

EXERCISE 1

1. Yesterday I went to a museum, where I learned a lot.

2. I learned that corals are animals.

3. I had always thought that they were plants.

4. I learned that there are 800,000 species of insects on earth.

5. That is more than if we counted all other animals and plants together.

6. Mammals are the only animals that suckle their young.

7. And bats are the only mammals that fly.

8. I learned more than I had expected to on that visit.

9. If you want to broaden your knowledge, you should go to a museum.

10. What you can learn is amazing.

EXERCISE 2

1. When a leaf falls from a tree
2. what I thought
3. that a leaf still has value
4. When it falls into a stream, that are called shredders
5. that eat the soft part of the leaf
6. that have eaten the leaf
7. that has eaten the shredders
8. who has not been lucky in his fishing
9. which is then eaten by his family
10. because it has become food for insects, fish, and also people

EXERCISE 3

1. When I go out on a dark evening
2. If I take the time
3. As the weeks go by
4. If I'm on campus in the evening
5. that I had taken my astronomy course sooner
6. that I had never imagined before
7. that may be the largest object in the universe
8. Whereas the Earth's diameter is about 8,000 miles
9. If you stood on the moon and looked back toward Earth
10. that you would see

EXERCISE 4

1. As he ran to catch the ball, he missed it.
2. Independent clause
3. Independent clause
4. Because no one had told me about the new ruling, I was late with my report.
5. When I finally decide to really work, I can accomplish a lot.
6. Independent clause
7. If I can just spend a couple of hours on my math, I can pass that test.
8. Independent clause
9. When I'm finished with both of them, I can relax.
10. Independent clause

EXERCISE 5

1. Last summer a friend and I took a trip across western Canada because we . . .
2. We drove from Winnipeg to Vancouver, which was . . .
3. We saw many interesting things that we'll not soon forget.

4. The most interesting of all was the Tyrrell Museum of Paleontology, which is . . .
5. I have now learned the meaning of *paleontology*, which is the . . .
6. The museum is named for Joseph B. Tyrrell, who discovered . . .
7. Tyrrell was a geologist who was . . .
8. One day in 1884 when he was looking for veins of coal, he accidentally . . .
9. The museum was opened in 1985 and contains thirty-five complete dinosaur skeletons, which is . . .
10. Now we can learn about dinosaurs, which roamed . . .

EXERCISE 6

1. In the Tyrrell Museum we learned about 3.5 million years of the Earth's history, which extends . . .
2. The most striking thing about the dinosaurs in Alberta is their lifestyles, which were . . .
3. Some dinosaurs laid eggs while some . . .
4. Some migrated as far as two thousand miles a year while others . . .
5. Some were cold-blooded while some . . .
6. An indoor garden in the museum houses 110 species of plants that are . . .
7. Some of the plants merely resemble those of dinosaur times while others . . .
8. More than half a million people annually visit the museum, which is . . .
9. Although we learned much about dinosaurs during our day there, we left . . .
10. The next day, as we continued our trip, we . . .

EXERCISE 7

1. When people have 20/20 vision, . . .
2. Although such vision is perfect for humans, . . .
3. Some birds have vision that may be sharper than that of humans.
4. If a hawk were perched on top of the Empire State Building, . . .
5. Since a hawk has vision eight times greater than that of humans, . . .
6. Because a frog has a different kind of vision, . . .
7. The cells in a frog's eyes have been called bug detectors because they respond mainly to moving objects.
8. The frog sees the tiny movement of bugs that the human eye could not detect.
9. But if a frog were sitting in a field of dead bugs, . . .
10. Although human eyesight is rather limited compared to that of other species, . . .

EXERCISE 8

1. Although we think of apples as food for people, . . .
2. Since bears are led by their sense of smell, . . .
3. Apple leaves are eaten by deer whereas apple seeds . . .
4. Because birds also eat young apple buds, apple growers have been . . .
5. Now most apple growers accept the debudding because it actually . . .
6. Although some trees hold their fruit all winter, . . .
7. When the apples on the ground rot, . . .
8. Since worms flourish in the enriched soil, . . .
9. When a nineteenth-century missionary from Massachusetts traveled across the country, . . .
10. As the news of John Chapman's work spread, . . .

EXERCISE 9

1. Although Thoreau said in 1854, . . .
2. Then in the 1950s a plan was proposed to set aside vast tracts of public lands where wildlife . . .
3. Because the proposed Wilderness Act set off a bitter seven-year struggle in Congress . . .
4. When finally the Wilderness Act of 1964 was passed, . . .
5. Because public support grew, . . .
6. Although opponents of the act said it would deprive the country of mineral and timber resources, . . .
7. While the unspoiled wilderness has tremendous economic value for recreation and tourism, . . .
8. Because the Wilderness Act of 1964 began the environmental movement, . . .
9. There are still many areas to be preserved, such as more than 12 million acres surrounding Yellowstone Park, which include . . .
10. Although more than 90 million acres are now protected, . . .

More about Fragments (p. 87)

EXERCISE 1

1. After answering the telephone and taking the message, she left.
2. (sentence)
3. After falling on the ice and breaking his leg, he could no longer compete.
4. The announcement that there would be no classes on Friday was welcome.
5. (sentence)
6. I don't know whether . . .
7. My parents want . . .

8. Not wanting to disappoint them, I made the effort to go.
9. My father is . . .
10. Having always done his best in school, he graduated with honors.

EXERCISE 2

1. We had walked . . .
2. We walked where . . .
3. Trying to keep the fire burning, we gathered more wood.
4. (sentence)
5. Having traveled almost two hundred miles, we were weary.
6. It was a boring . . .
7. I had nothing to do . . .
8. Her family enjoyed the gracious . . .
9. She needed a place . . .
10. She finished the day . . .

EXERCISE 3

Individuals can help save our forests. Americans waste vast amounts of paper because they don't think of paper as forests. They think nothing of wasting an envelope because an envelope is only a tiny piece of paper, but it takes 2 million trees to make the yearly supply of 112 billion envelopes. Even small savings can encourage others to save until finally the concerted efforts of enough individuals can make a difference.

Review of Run-Together Sentences and Fragments (p. 90)

1. The science of medicine has had a long history. It began with superstitions, and illness was attributed to evil spirits. The ancient Egyptians were among the first to practice surgery. Anesthesia was, of course, unknown. Therefore the patient was made unconscious by a blow on the head with a mallet. Surgery was also practiced in early Babylonia, and the Code of Hammurabi lists the penalties that an unsuccessful surgeon had to pay. For example, if a patient lost an eye through poor surgery, the surgeon's hand was cut off.

2. In 1598 the famous Globe Theater was built across the Thames from London. Shakespeare became a shareholder, and his plays were produced there. The theater was octagonal and held about twelve hundred people. The "groundlings" stood on the floor and watched the play, but the wealthier patrons sat in the two galleries. Those paying the highest fees could sit on the stage. The stage jutted out into the audience; thus the players and the audience had a close relationship.

Using Standard English Verbs (p. 94)

EXERCISE 1

1. walk, walked
2. am, was
3. has, had
4. do, did
5. needs, needed
6. helps, helped
7. want, wanted
8. attends, attended
9. talks, talked
10. suppose, supposed

EXERCISE 2

1. am, was
2. do, did
3. has, had
4. ask, asked
5. enjoy, enjoyed
6. finishes, finished
7. learns, learned
8. works, worked
9. listen, listened
10. play, played

EXERCISE 3

1. joined, like
2. played, play
3. needs, hopes
4. doesn't, is
5. work, learn
6. expects, insists
7. practice, have
8. enjoys, benefits
9. watch, do
10. were, praised

EXERCISE 4

1. liked, work
2. learned, discussed
3. explained, did
4. do, hope
5. liked, dropped
6. checked, decided
7. picked, did
8. encouraged, listened
9. gets, is
10. advises, treats

EXERCISE 5

1. traveled
2. boarded
3. were
4. learned
5. surprised, was
6. was glad
7. had
8. liked
9. walked, tried
10. learned

Using Helping Verbs and Irregular Verbs (p. 101)

EXERCISE 1

1. finish, finished
2. finish
3. finished, finish
4. finishing
5. finished
6. finished
7. finish
8. finished
9. finish
10. finished

EXERCISE 2

1. speak, begun
2. seems, want
3. know, become
4. imitating, use
5. teach, beginning
6. like
7. spoken, learned
8. intend, began
9. were, realized
10. helped, were, beginning

EXERCISE 3

1. were, saw
2. seen, begun
3. driven, eaten
4. offered, did
5. ate, asked
6. written, asked, received
7. come, begun
8. saw, suggested
9. gone, washed, prepared
10. saw, were, drove

EXERCISE 4

1. decided, seen
2. frozen, reached
3. was, come
4. observed, saw
5. announced, won
6. smiled, received
7. were, done
8. Were, accepted
9. went, congratulated
10. plans, intends

Avoiding Dialect Expressions (p. 105)

EXERCISE 1

1. sister did well
2. I was no good at sports, and anyway I haven't got time for them.
3. brother was no expert
4. fix his car himself . . . how to fix it well.
5. that has no sense.
6. dog runs somewhere . . . it doesn't come
7. I have never understood
8. dog is friendly.
9. This book was assigned reading.
10. I am finished

EXERCISE 2

1. somewhere
2. I have nothing . . . and anyway I
3. Anywhere I am going
4. my brother always wants to stop somewhere
5. I haven't any money.
6. Mom is fixing
7. mom is
8. parents are
9. that computer and those books.
10. haven't ever asked

Progress Test (p. 107)

1. B
2. A
3. B
4. A
5. B
6. B
7. A
8. A
9. A
10. B
11. B
12. B
13. A
14. B
15. B

Making Subjects, Verbs, and Pronouns Agree (p. 110)

EXERCISE 1

1. is
2. is
3. is
4. doesn't
5. is, his
6. were
7. doesn't
8. wants
9. think
10. intend

EXERCISE 2

1. is
2. helps
3. are
4. has
5. were, were
6. depends
7. doesn't
8. work
9. requires
10. is

EXERCISE 3

1. is
2. has
3. feel
4. wants
5. like
6. has
7. is, wants
8. doesn't
9. follow
10. doesn't

EXERCISE 4

1. has, have
2. have
3. have, is
4. have, has
5. is

6. want
7. vary
8. has
9. wants, are
10. is

Choosing the Right Pronoun (p. 113)

EXERCISE 1

1. me
2. me
3. him and me
4. he and I
5. us

6. I am
7. he does
8. he and I
9. I
10. he, I

EXERCISE 2

1. I
2. me
3. we
4. he and I
5. we

6. me
7. me
8. he and I
9. I
10. us

EXERCISE 3

1. I
2. him and me
3. us
4. me
5. I

6. I
7. I
8. he and I
9. we
10. he and I

EXERCISE 4

1. David and I
2. us
3. he and I
4. I
5. me

6. We
7. he and I
8. me
9. David and I
10. me

Making the Pronoun Refer to the Right Word (p. 116)

EXERCISE 1

1. I put the omelet on the table, took off my apron, and began to eat.
2. I was pleased that they offered me a job.
3. Trying to decide what trip to take isn't easy.
4. She said to her sister, "My room is a mess."
5. I have a pair of glasses, but my eyes are so good that I don't use the glasses except for reading.
6. The president said to the dean, "You have been too lenient."
7. The child was pleased when I praised the finger painting.
8. I thought he would phone, and I waited all evening for the phone to ring.
9. The teachers arranged for a play center where the children can play on swings, slides, and jungle gyms.
10. Felipe said to the professor, "Your watch is wrong."

EXERCISE 2

1. We couldn't find the cake plate and realized the children must have eaten the cake.
2. He told his dad, "You need a new suit."
3. As I approached the baby's playpen, the baby began to cry.
4. The child screamed when I moved the tricycle.
5. After I read about Lindbergh's life, I decided I wanted to be an airline pilot.
6. As soon as the fender was repaired, I drove the car home.
7. The sentence is correct.
8. When I opened the door of the kennel, the dog ran away.
9. We couldn't find a single can and blamed Rudy for drinking the colas.
10. His motorcycle swerved into the side of the house, but the bike wasn't damaged.

EXERCISE 3

1. The dog barked while I was holding its water dish.
2. I was pleased that they offered me a job.
3. It isn't easy to decide what trip to take.
4. She said that her sister's room was a mess.
5. The sentence is correct.
6. Ellen said that the riding instructor's horse needed to be brushed.
7. The shark swam away when I tapped on its aquarium.
8. His parents were disappointed that he told the lawyer about the case.
9. The sentence is correct.
10. Jill told her sister, "Call again when I'm not so busy."

EXERCISE 4

1. The dog began to whine when I picked up its dish.
2. I have been interested in coaching football ever since I was in high school, and now I have decided to become a coach.
3. My family was annoyed that I decided not to accept the summer job.
4. She asked her sister, "Why wasn't I invited to the party?"
5. Jay's father said, "You can take your new tennis racket to school."
6. I have always liked French Provencial furniture and have finally decided to buy some.
7. She told her instructor, "I don't understand what you are saying."
8. She likes to swim and spends most of her summer swimming.
9. She is not very good in sports. But she is good in her studies and this is why she was chosen student body president.
10. Ed was really despondent when the boss talked to him.

EXERCISE 5

1. Because I enjoy teaching I would like to be a teacher.
2. My bicycle wasn't damaged when it hit the car.
3. Fred told his cousin, "My dog has run away."
4. She couldn't run fast, but she received the award because she was an excellent swimmer.
5. The instructor told him, "Your typewriter needs a new ribbon."
6. He told his father, "You ought to wash the car."
7. I walked into the room, climbed on the ladder, and began to paint the room.
8. The sentence is correct.
9. She told her mother, "I need to be positive before making such a big decision."
10. Sarah told her sister, "You need to wash the car."

EXERCISE 6

1. Andy told his brother, "My car had a flat tire."
2. I don't like the cold in New England at this time of year.
3. She asked the mechanic, "Why are you having trouble?"
4. Her sister was crying when she came in at 4 A.M.
5. The dog ran away as I tried to attach its leash.
6. The sentence is correct.
7. The drivers didn't even look my way as the cars whizzed past.
8. The robin flew away as I approached its nest.
9. It won't be easy for me to save all my money for a trip.
10. She told her daughter, "I missed my appointment."

EXERCISE 7

1. The kitten ran off as soon as its paw was bandaged.
2. His brother said, "You are a good tennis player."
3. She served me cold pizza.
4. I learned the easy card trick.
5. I have adjusted the steering wheel and you can take the car home.
6. Sam was almost hit by a football as he walked toward the coach.
7. He told the man, "Come back when you have time to talk."
8. Jerome was angry when he talked to his father.
9. Ben told his father, "You ought to get a refund for the faulty tire."
10. The rabbit ran away when I opened the door of its cage.

Correcting Misplaced or Dangling Modifiers (p. 121)

EXERCISE 1

1. While I talked on the phone, the cake . . .
2. I came across my grandfather sound . . .
3. I saw a furry little caterpillar crawling . . .
4. As he took her in his arms, the moon . . .
5. Years later you will . . .
6. The sentence is correct.
7. Lincoln Park is the most interesting park I have seen in the city.
8. She was engaged to a man named Victor, who had a . . .
9. When I was 14, my . . .
10. We gave all the food we didn't want to . . .

EXERCISE 2

1. After I had cleaned my room, my dog . . .
2. A son weighing eight pounds was . . .
3. I don't enjoy his company because he's . . .
4. I don't care for cucumbers unless they are pickled.
5. I tried to quiet the screaming and kicking child.
6. The car I bought from a used-car dealer had a . . .
7. I saw the broken ladder leaning . . .
8. After watching TV all evening, I found the dirty dishes . . .
9. When I was six, my . . .
10. The sentence is correct.

EXERCISE 3

1. While tobogganing down the hill, we saw a huge bear come into view.
2. On the way to school I saw . . .
3. He thought she looked elegant dressed in a pink satin dinner dress.
4. Because I had gone to too many parties, my . . .
5. The series of lectures we are having on religions of the world will . . .

Using Parallel Construction (p. 126)

EXERCISE 1

1. and sleeping late . . .
2. and by taking him . . .
3. or giving an oral report.
4. The sentence is correct.
5. and an old popcorn popper.
6. than to have a great . . .
7. The sentence is correct.
8. 90 feet deep.
9. The sentence is correct.
10. The sentence is correct.

EXERCISE 2

1. masonry, and even concrete and metals.
2. The sentence is correct.
3. rain, or even snow.
4. blossoms waving . . .
5. and to kill pain.
6. And then decorates it . . .
   and sometimes pinecones stuffed with suet.
7. The sentence is correct.

EXERCISE 3

1. Every college student should know how to type.
   1. Some instructors require typed papers.
   2. Typing, if one is good at it, saves time.
   3. A typed paper often gets a higher grade.
2. Going home every weekend is unwise.
   1. I spend too much time on the bus.
   2. I get behind in my college work.
   3. It is too expensive.
   4. I miss out on weekend activities at college.

Correcting Shift in Time (p. 129)

EXERCISE 1

My mother stood . . . because she was afraid I was going to fall off the roof. In spite of her I finally got it up . . . I was listening . . . Eventually I decided I wanted . . . Mostly I just listened and worked . . .

EXERCISE 2

. . . Also, she said, they slobber . . . She said people don't like to admit . . .

EXERCISE 3

. . . he decided that the routine of study was . . . he tramped, taught school, made shoes, and edited . . . he was writing poetry . . . he found himself famous.

Correcting Shift in Person (p. 133)

EXERCISE 1

. . . I want you." Watson rushed . . .

EXERCISE 2

. . . . It's as if a person cut off an arm and a new one grew.

EXERCISE 3

But compared with the pace of Variegated Glacier . . .

EXERCISE 4

Of course I wouldn't really want a dead tree on my . . . So a tree's life isn't over . . . decomposes, insects lay their eggs in its spongy wood.

EXERCISE 5

It was my sign of independence. It was my ticket to freedom. I didn't have to ask to borrow the family car, and I didn't have to explain where I was going or when I'd be back . . . every accessory imaginable . . . Funny how it costs freedom to support freedom.

Correcting Wordiness (p. 137)

EXERCISE 1

1. I woke up at four this morning.
2. We were considering whether to charge admission.
3. Many people never read a book.
4. After our eight-hour hike, we were hungry.
5. He had tried football, basketball, and hockey.
6. He can be depended upon to do what he says he will.
7. I was surprised yesterday when my college roommate stopped to see me.
8. I think she's planning to go.
9. I had no money by the end of the year.
10. The three kinds of stones we found were unique.

EXERCISE 2

1. No doubt our team will win.
2. They carried him home drunk.
3. There is more permissiveness today than formerly.
4. Justice is too slow in our country.
5. Justice should be swift and sure.
6. Planning for the trip was left up to Mike and me.

7. His height makes him a good basketball player.
8. The melons were large and sweet.
9. Most students don't leave campus on weekends.
10. Finally one should learn more at college than what is learned in courses.

EXERCISE 3

1. Most people spend too much time watching TV.
2. I forgot about last night's meeting.
3. Most writers use too many words.
4. A new car should not be driven too fast for the first five hundred miles.
5. I'm happy to accept your invitation.
6. I intend to finish my year here and then look for a job.
7. Most people want a clear, concise business form.
8. The president should bring the motion to a vote.
9. I thought she was just pretending to be ill.
10. I'm trying to get rid of wordiness in my papers.

EXERCISE 4

To help new students find their way around the Library, the staff offers orientation programs. Many faculty members also bring their classes to particular subject areas for orientation. And printed handouts, such as special subject bibliographies, how to do computer searches, and instructions for using microfilm, periodical indexes and psychological abstracts, are available.

Avoiding Clichés (p. 140)

EXERCISE 1

1. Since I hadn't opened a book all weekend, I decided to do a little studying before I went to bed.
2. Then I changed my mind.
3. I decided I'd rather do some cooking.
4. Therefore I went to the kitchen and got out my equipment.
5. But there were no eggs in the fridge and no cake mix in the cupboard.
6. I didn't know what to do.
7. Since I couldn't find any ingredients, I decided to clean the kitchen.
8. I worked hard and soon had everything clean.
9. But finally I decided to do some studying.
10. I studied late that night, but the next morning I was up early and ready for my exam.

Review of Sentence Structure (p. 142)

1. B	6. B	11. B	16. B	21. A
2. A	7. A	12. A	17. B	22. A
3. A	8. B	13. A	18. A	23. B
4. B	9. B	14. B	19. A	24. A
5. B	10. B	15. A	20. B	25. B

Punctuation (p. 148)

EXERCISE 1

1. bus. We
2. equipment:
3. The sentence is correct.
4. Placid. We'd
5. beautiful. We
6. there. The
7. crusty. It
8. week. I'll
9. best:
10. Placid. It

EXERCISE 2

1. following materials:
2. out. He
3. shed.
4. appeared. By
5. 1924. A
6. States. That
7. competition. Then
8. compacts.
9. advantages:
10. Japanese;

EXERCISE 3

1. Michigan?
2. village. It's
3. past. Then
4. Dearborn. Then
5. carriage. Next
6. great;
7. The sentence is correct.
8. buildings. He
9. museum. One
10. life. Ford

EXERCISE 4

1. pencils. Now
2. tail." From
3. discovered. People
4. twine; then
5. Germany. It
6. pencils. Conté
7. dry. His
8. 1827. Now
9. pencils. Pencils
10. The sentence is correct.

EXERCISE 5

1. player. Then
2. up. He
3. 1980. His
4. leg. Some
5. weather:
6. perseverance. They
7. him. He
8. up. The
9. miles. Furthermore
10. point.

EXERCISE 6

1. metric?
2. three:
3. started?
4. The sentence is correct.
5. 1970s.
6. kilometers. Gas
7. change. In
8. signs. Industry
9. Arabia. The
10. system. The

EXERCISE 7

1. farms?
2. energy. Now
3. jobs:
4. soil;
5. morning. Tractors
6. years. The
7. itself. Other
8. food;
9. can. However
10. farms. They

EXERCISE 8

1. metric. Even
2. speedometers). Ford
3. systems; yards
4. products. They
5. complicated. Soon
6. way; social
7. metric. It
8. The sentence is correct.
9. schools. The
10. management. Then

Commas (p. 154)

EXERCISE 1

1. trip,
2. brochures,
3. time,
4. newspapers, encyclopedias,
5. Yes, planning . . . travel,
6. away,
7. planning,
8. college,
9. Hawaii, Tahiti,
10. far,

EXERCISE 2

1. lately,
2. years,
3. dull,
4. lecture,
5. me,
6. daydreaming,
7. off,
8. The sentence is correct.
9. marks,
10. all,

EXERCISE 3

1. animal,
2. 1800s,
3. West,
4. settlers, by sportsmen,
5. supply,
6. States,
7. management, the . . . comeback,
8. Yellowstone National Park, National Bison Range in Montana,
9. free,
10. heritage,

EXERCISE 4

1. States,
2. Maine, Shenandoah in Virginia, Mammoth Cave in Kentucky, Great Smokey Mountains in Tennessee and North Carolina, and the Everglades, Biscayne and Dry Tortugas in Florida.
3. The sentence is correct.
4. summer,
5. stalagmites,
6. cave,
7. water,
8. purple, brown,
9. cave,
10. levels,

EXERCISE 5

1. River, Frozen Niagara,
2. left,
3. parks,
4. acres,
5. created,
6. geysers, hot springs, lakes, rivers,
7. Yellowstone,
8. 1870,
9. nature,
10. prohibited,

EXERCISE 6

1. hour,
2. "swift creature,"
3. delicate,
4. today,
5. measured,
6. head,
7. leaves, twigs,
8. branch, draws . . . lips,
9. acacia,
10. The sentence is correct.

EXERCISE 7

1. harm,
2. anyone,
3. eat,
4. animals,
5. world,
6. ignored, and . . . chips, bread, cheese,
7. animals,
8. The sentence is correct.
9. laws,
10. thoughtlessness,

EXERCISE 8

1. skiing,
2. it,
3. skiing,
4. slalom, giant slalom, and downhill
5. States,
6. two,
7. The sentence is correct.
8. The sentence is correct.
9. with,
10. ambitious,

EXERCISE 9

1. article,
2. feet,
3. wild,
4. extinction,
5. species,

6. existed, . . . captured,
7. First,
8. Second, . . . hunters,
9. Third, . . . passed,
10. habitat,

EXERCISE 10

1. young,
2. nests,
3. evenly,
4. hisses, grunts, . . . heard,
5. last,

6. condor,
7. pounds,
8. years,
9. survival,
10. wild,

Commas (continued) (p. 162)

EXERCISE 1

1. The sentence is correct.
2. suit, which . . . Easter,
3. The sentence is correct.
4. Atchison, where . . . up,
5. The sentence is correct.

6. chair, which
7. Kilauea, which . . . Hawaii,
8. The sentence is correct.
9. Queen City, where . . . ago,
10. The sentence is correct.

EXERCISE 2

1. The sentence is correct.
2. house, which . . . built,
3. wife, who . . . kindergarten,
4. Sybil, who . . . kindergarten,
5. The sentence is correct.

6. Sims, who . . . night,
7. Camaro, which . . . ago,
8. The sentence is correct.
9. The sentence is correct.
10. dad, who . . . football,

EXERCISE 3

1. Jason, who . . . asleep,
2. was, of course,
3. paper, however,
4. The sentence is correct.
5. paper, I know,

6. think, Connie,
7. writing, which . . . lately,
8. rewriting, of course,
9. The sentence is correct.
10. Rewrite, our . . . says,

EXERCISE 4

1. people, I find,
2. weeks, which . . . vacation,
3. colors, which . . . city,
4. can't, I think,
5. city, which . . . Superior,

6. Superior, which . . . deep,
7. Bridge,
8. span, which . . . tons,
9. Depot,
10. museums,

EXERCISE 5

1. Jorge, who's . . . friend,
2. days, of course,
3. Park,
4. and, furthermore,
5. decided, therefore,
6. glaciers,
7. Glacier,
8. was, beyond a doubt,
9. naturalist, who . . . the glacier,
10. movement, he explained,

EXERCISE 6

1. East, which . . . weather,
2. systems, which . . . ones,
3. provide, obviously,
4. able, furthermore,
5. Vermont, which . . . lifts,
6. Vermont, which . . . year,
7. systems, however,
8. The sentence is correct.
9. surprising, therefore,
10. money, beyond a doubt,

EXERCISE 7

1. Rankin, who . . . $700,
2. Rankin, a . . . Montana,
3. 1917, therefore,
4. told, furthermore,
5. voted, nevertheless,
6. War, she said,
7. Harbor, which . . . war,
8. White, editor . . . *Emporia Gazette,*
9. Kennedy, writing . . . later,
10. The sentence is correct.

Review of the Comma (p. 166)

1. Highway 1,
2. The sentence is correct.
3. keys, which . . . Florida,
4. collecting, bird-watching,
5. collectors, who . . . shells,
6. herons, pelicans,
7. people,
8. abound,
9. The sentence is correct.
10. Center,
11. keys, the most . . . Deer,
12. highways, and . . . year,
13. Audubon, Hart Crane,

Quotation Marks (p. 169)

EXERCISE 1

1. "Let's get something to eat,"
2. "Do you want to go now or after the movie?"
3. "Why not both times?"
4. "Snow and adolescence are the only problems that disappear if you ignore them long enough,"

5. "Some people can stay longer in an hour than others can in a week,"
6. The sentence is correct.
7. "If people could be got into the woods, even for once," John Muir said, "to hear the trees speak for themselves, all difficulties in the way of forest preservation would vanish."
8. "With all its sham, drudgery, and broken dreams," said Adlai Stevenson, "it is still a beautiful world."
9. We went to see *The Wild Duck,*
10. "Our future as a nation is going to depend not so much on what happens in outer space as on what happens in inner space—the space between our ears,"

EXERCISE 2

1. "The actions of some children," said Will Rogers "suggest that their parents embarked on the sea of matrimony without a paddle."
2. "The best time to tackle a small problem," said my father, "is before he grows up."
3. "When Mom goes shopping," says Kip, "she leaves no store unturned."
4. I agree with the Spanish proverb "How beautiful it is to do nothing and then rest afterward."
5. He found her munching chocolates and reading a book entitled *Eat, Drink, and Be Buried.*
6. Mark Twain said, "When I was a boy of 14, my father was so ignorant I could hardly stand to have the old man around. But when I got to be 21, I was astonished at how much the old man had learned in seven years."
7. Mark Twain said, "The parts of the Bible which give me the most trouble are those I understand the best."
8. "Work consists of whatever a body is obliged to do, and play consists of whatever a body is not obliged to do,"
9. On observing the great number of civic statues, Cato, a famous Roman, remarked, "I would rather people would ask why there is not a statue of Cato than why there is."
10. "One does not complain about water because it is wet," said Abraham Maslow, "nor about rocks because they are hard."

EXERCISE 3

1. "I've just read "Barn Burning,"
2. "The construction of an airplane," wrote Charles Lindbergh, "is simple compared to the evolutionary achievement of a bird."
3. "If I had the choice," Lindbergh continued, "I would rather have birds than airplanes."
4. The sentence is correct.
5. The sentence is correct.

6. He said, "People say I play as easily as a bird sings. If they only knew how much effort their bird has put into his song."
7. "As it is the mark of great minds to say many things in a few words," wrote La Rochefoucauld, "so it is the mark of little minds to use many words to say nothing."
8. The sentence is correct.
9. "Whatever you have you must either use or lose,"
10. "A span of time either leaves you better off or worse off," wrote John Gardner. "There is no neutral time."

EXERCISE 4

1. "Finish every day and be done with it," said Ralph Waldo Emerson. "Tomorrow is a new day."
2. "Life can only be understood backward," said Kierkegaard, "but it must be lived forward."
3. "The most valuable of all talents is that of never using two words when one will do,"
4. "The only conquests that are permanent and leave no regrets," Napoleon said, "are our conquests over ourselves."
5. "Nearly all men can stand adversity, but if you want to test a man's character, give him power,"
6. The sentence is correct.
7. In the novel *Fathers and Sons*
8. "Nobody can carry three watermelons under one arm,"
9. "The taller the bamboo grows the lower it bends,"
10. "The man who does not do more work than he's paid for," said Abraham Lincoln, "isn't worth what he gets."

EXERCISE 5

1. "The cost of a thing is the amount of what I call life which is required to be exchanged for it, immediately or in the long run,"
2. "A man is rich," said Thoreau, "in proportion to the number of things he can afford to let alone."
3. Viewing the multitude of articles exposed for sale in the marketplace, Socrates remarked, "How many things there are that I do not want."
4. "What! Sell land?" said Tecumseh, a Shawnee Indian chief. "As well sell air and water. The Great Spirit gave them in common to all—the air to breathe, the water to drink, and the land to live upon."
5. "Perhaps the most valuable result of all education," said Thomas Huxley, "is the ability to make yourself do the thing you have to do, when it ought to be done, whether you like it or not."
6. The sentence is correct.
7. "Education does not mean teaching people to know what they do not know," said John Ruskin. "It means teaching them to behave as they do not behave."

8. "Sometimes when fate kicks us and we finally land and look around, we find we have been kicked upstairs,"

EXERCISE 6

1. "By the year 2000, if present trends continue," said the professor, "the world will be losing one plant or animal species every hour of every day."
2. "What's so important," a student asked, "about the extinction of a pupfish or a coneflower?"
3. "It may be of immense importance!" the professor continued. "Half of our modern medicines, for example, can be traced to wild organisms."
4. "And I suppose wild plants could give us more medicines,"
5. "Right," said the professor. "The source for our next miracle drug could be one of the plants that are endangered right now."
6. "What can we do about it?"
7. The sentence is correct.

Capital Letters (p. 175)

EXERCISE 1

1. Junior College, Labor Day
2. English, Spanish
3. English
4. The sentence is correct.
5. "The Death of the Hired Man"
6. "A Worn Path"
7. The sentence is correct.
8. English
9. High School
10. Psychology 101, History 210 . . . Spanish

EXERCISE 2

1. The sentence is correct.
2. Fourth
3. The sentence is correct.
4. East
5. The sentence is correct.
6. Park
7. Mom, Dad, Lake Superior
8. Dunes State Park
9. The sentence is correct.
10. Cassiopeia, Orion

EXERCISE 3

1. The sentence is correct.
2. River
3. Granddad
4. The sentence is correct.
5. River Lake
6. Granddad
7. The sentence is correct.
8. State College
9. The sentence is correct.
10. The sentence is correct.

EXERCISE 4

1. *Newsweek*
2. Lung Association
3. Tobacco Company
4. United States
5. The sentence is correct.
6. The sentence is correct.
7. The sentence is correct.
8. Lung Association
9. Aren't
10. It's

EXERCISE 5

1. The sentence is correct.
2. The sentence is correct.
3. Junior College
4. The sentence is correct.
5. University
6. The sentence is correct.
7. The sentence is correct.
8. The sentence is correct.
9. The sentence is correct.
10. The sentence is correct.

EXERCISE 6

1. Yukon
2. The sentence is correct.
3. Park
4. Lake of the Woods
5. The sentence is correct.
6. The sentence is correct.
7. Aunt
8. The sentence is correct.
9. The sentence is correct.
10. The sentence is correct.

EXERCISE 7

1. The sentence is correct.
2. *Time* and *Newsweek* . . . *The Smithsonian*
3. "Life for Lefties."
4. The sentence is correct.
5. The sentence is correct.
6. The sentence is correct.
7. The sentence is correct.
8. The sentence is correct.
9. Presidents
10. The sentence is correct.

EXERCISE 8

1. Midwest, West
2. Dad
3. Red River
4. Mount
5. National Park
6. The sentence is correct.
7. The sentence is correct.
8. Mother, Dad, Ocean
9. County, Golden Gate Bridge
10. West Coast, East

EXERCISE 9

1. The sentence is correct.
2. City College
3. Motor Company
4. Oil Company
5. The sentence is correct.
6. Dad
7. Dad
8. "How to Buy Your First Motorcycle"
9. The sentence is correct.
10. The sentence is correct.

Review of Punctuation and Capital Letters (p. 179)

EXERCISE 1

1. The Taj Mahal, which is in Agra,
2. Do you read *Time* or *Newsweek*?
3. I'm glad it's snowing;
4. Skiing, skating,
5. Figure skating, which I'm just learning,
6. His knapsack contained the following items: food, matches,
7. The sign in the dentist's office read, "Support your dentist. Eat candy."
8. Sydney J. Harris says, "It seems to me that growing older imposes a duty upon us to get more like a peach on the inside as we get more like a prune on the outside."
9. A little old lady from Boston refused to travel saying, "Why should I travel? I'm already here."
10. You can get the document by writing to the Superintendent of Documents, Government Printing Office, Washington,
11. My mother, who is not a writer herself,
12. He tried to improve his vocabulary by looking up new words, by keeping word lists,
13. "Children have never been good at listening to their elders," says James Baldwin, "but they have never failed to imitate them."
14. Reading improves your understanding of human nature;
15. One tree can make three million matches;
16. An Arabian proverb says, "I had no shoes and complained until I met a man who had no feet."

Proofreading

EXERCISE 1 (p. 182)

straight-forward; all I
I don't know what
the men there first thought
radio, but
but I knew it
it finished.
My wiring didn't
explanation. I was
if I'd invented

EXERCISE 2 (p. 183)

Sometimes I'd last a month, and sometimes only a day or two.
want to stop. I was one
~~control myself. I was~~
wanted me to do. It was then

EXERCISE 3 (p. 184)

rafting before, and it
was supposed to
to head, but already
It's an amazing
turned around, but then
we both happened to lean
raft tipping sideways

Comprehensive Test (p. 185)

1. ~~Its~~ *It's* useless to wait. ~~hes~~ *He's* probably not coming.

2. If one wants a larger vocabulary, ~~you~~ *one* should study word roots.

3. ~~Spending~~ *I spent* entirely too much time on that one ~~coarse~~ *course* last semester.

4. Dad ~~ask~~ *asked* my sister and me to water the lawn. ~~we was~~ *We were* glad to do it.

5. While they were waiting for ~~there~~ *their* daughter, ~~they're~~ *their* engine stalled.

6. I ~~cant~~ *can't* decide whether to finish my math, study my history, or ~~whether I~~

   ~~should~~ take it easy for a change.

7. If you're going to be ~~hear~~ *here*, Dawn, you can answer the phone for me.

8. ~~Your~~ *You're* going with me, aren't you~~.~~?

9. We freshmen helped ~~a~~ *an* upperclass student with registration. ~~he~~ *He* really

   appreciated it.

10. I was ~~quiet~~ _quite_ sure that ~~Rons~~ _Ron's_ car was in the driveway.

11. When we were on our trip, we visited some cities in the ~~south~~ _South_.

12. ~~Which~~ _The cities_ had many beautiful old homes and lovely gardens.

13. ~~Its~~ _It's_ Mr. Peterson's car, but ~~hes~~ _he's_ not driving it.

14. Each of the students ~~are~~ _is_ planning ~~a~~ _an_ individual report.

15. Looking under the car, _we found_ the missing baseball. ~~was found~~

16. ~~Christines~~ _Christine's_ grades are always higher than ~~Elizabeths~~ _Elizabeth's_.

17. ~~Ill~~ _"I'll_ be ready in a minute," Jeanne said.

18. This semester I'm taking ~~french~~ _French_, history, and ~~english~~ _English_.

19. The ~~united nations~~ _United Nations_ receives more brickbats than bravos, yet it remains

    the only real hope for peace.

20. She ~~told~~ _said to_ her sister, _"I need_ ~~she needed~~ a new purse."

21. They ~~didnt~~ _didn't_ think, however, that they would have time to come back.

22. She was ~~suppose~~ _supposed_ to read the short story "The Elephant's Child" from

    Rudyard Kipling's book Just So Stories.

23. ~~Whether~~ _I don't care whether_ you agree with me or whether you follow your own ideas.

24. We waited as long as we could. ~~than~~ _Then_ we went on without her.

25. ~~Whats~~ _"What's_ done to children, they will do to society," wrote Karl Menninger.

Writing

EXERCISE 1 (p. 194)

2, 3, 4, 5, 6, 8, 9 should be marked THESIS.

EXERCISE 2 (p. 195)

I've decided not to quit college.
1. I'd have difficulty finding a job.
2. I'll get a better job later if I have a college degree.
3. I'm really benefiting from some of my courses.

Our house is a madhouse when we're leaving on a trip.
1. Everyone is shouting orders.
2. No one wants to do the breakfast dishes.
3. We can't fit all our luggage into the car.
4. No one can find the road map.

To increase your vocabulary, you need to take three steps.
1. Look up words that interest you.
2. Look for word roots to give you clues to meaning.
3. Use your new words in speaking and writing.

EXERCISE 3 (p. 200)

In the first place
Then too *or* Also
Also *or* Then too
Therefore

Summary of "Novel Ending for Book Bugs" (p. 207)

Book bugs have infested libraries for years, but now a solution has been found. When Yale was given some priceless medieval manuscripts crawling with insects, the librarians turned to the Head of the Department of entomology. On a hunch, he put some of the bugs on ice. They were dead in a day and a half. Then he and the librarians put all the medieval manuscripts in a dining hall deep freeze for three days at minus forty degrees Fahrenheit. The books were then completely bug free. Now libraries across the country are installing walk-through freezers for their infested books.

Index